Fred Archer has written, among other books, *By Hook and By Crook*, *The Distant Scene*, *Poacher's Pie*, *A Lad of Evesham Vale* and *Golden Sheaves, Black Horses*.

Sally Seymour is a potter and an illustrator. Amongst other titles, she has illustrated *Self-Sufficiency* and *The Lore of The Land*.

FRED ARCHER
Farmer's Son

Pan Books London and Sydney

First published 1984 by Whittet Books Ltd
This edition published 1986 by Pan Books Ltd
Cavaye Place, London SW10 9PG
9 8 7 6 5 4 3 2 1
© Fred Archer 1984
ISBN 0 330 29199 8
Printed and bound in Great Britain by
Cox & Wyman Ltd, Reading

Contents

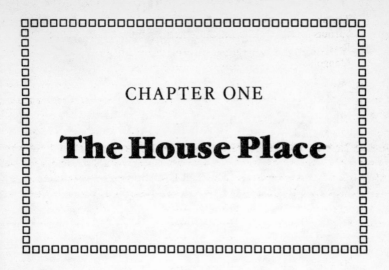

CHAPTER ONE

The House Place

If you have ever known the cosy harbour of a farmhouse fireside, you will appreciate the magic of sitting in one's green drill knickers and sailor suit with Mother, Dad, Grandad and Grandma in the inglenook, with the oil lamp hanging chained from the beams, casting light which shone golden, lighting half the room. Over by the china cupboard in the far corner shadows flickered against the flowered wallpaper. The walnut veneered piano with two brass candlesticks caught the very last rays from the lamp, as the twilight had some hours before it changed the garden yew tree to gold.

The fire itself sparked blue stars from the hawthorn log. They clung to the fireback like glow worms. 'Another frost, Tom,' Grandad said to Dad as he sat in his oak armchair, making spills from newspaper and putting them tidily into an old green porcelain vase.

'Looks all like it according to the blue of the fire,' Dad replied.

Grandad was a little man with a happy face, an outdoor red face, crinkled like a Russet apple, creased and lined by eighty Christmases and eighty summer suns. He had a short clipped beard, snow white hair and wore a grey, four-buttoned jacket with wide collar over his white starched shirt front fastened with little studs. Around his neck he still wore a red-and-white

Stanley Farm

muffler. His gnarled hands were chapped brown and dry. His chair backed onto the door where, despite the green curtain, the draught from the hall made the hanging brass lamp with its long glass globe flicker like a dying candle.

It was a Friday night just before Christmas. The great iron pot hung from the pot hooks over the fire all ready for two boys' baths. Dad had carried the galvanized bath from the back kitchen and put it on the rug in front of the fire.

Under the ingle, flitches of bacon hung drying from the salting; yellow fat, pink lean. A sack of unused flour stood just inside the pantry door, an insurance, so they said, against famine when the menace of German submarines had been a reality and the war still raged in France. On hooks and nails under the tar-painted ingle, which shone like patent leather, little bags of seed hung above the salt box (a block of salt which hung in a box on the inglenook to keep dry), while on a shelf above Dad's chair were his cartridges, big boxes of one hundred Crimson Flash. His gun hung on two hooks from the blackened beam over the fireplace. The oven grate was polished with black lead every morning by Mrs Vale the charwoman.

Grandma sat in an enormous winged easy chair. It was as if the chair had been made especially to fit her frame. Grandma and her chair took up the whole of that side of the fireside. A farmhouse Queen Victoria of a woman in black shot silk dress, clasped at a high neck with a mother-of-pearl brooch, she was crocheting a pink jumper, the little yellow bone hook moving mechanically between her fingers.

The great iron pot boiled as Dad took it from the fire, emptying the water into the bath where he had poured an enamel bucket full of cold water from the tap in the back kitchen. Clouds of steam rose to the beamed ceiling. The lamp shone like the sun trying hard on a misty day to break through in early morning. Mother elbowed the hot water, pouring more cold into the bath until it was ready for my weekly Friday night public naked episode.

Grandad's chair, Dad's chair, were pulled back from the fire. Only Grandma stayed, her crocheting laid aside with my brother Tom on her knee. He was older, so that his turn in the bath came later. The Sunlight soap, the flannel, the towelling down in front of the audience was a bit public for me. First on went the flannel vest, then the striped winceyette sleeping suit, a boiler suit outfit all in one, and then to Grandma's knee for prayers, looking up as I did so to this ample body in shining black silk and the smell of moth balls and eucalyptus. Every breath she took, as her frame ebbed and flowed like a gentle tide, smelt of eucalyptus.

'Gentle Jesus meek and mild, Look upon a little child.' All went well until it came to 'Pity my simplicity.' I couldn't say it, but a whispered chant from my elders remedied that. Up the winding stairs Mother shepherded me to the little iron bedstead with brass knobs. She held an enamelled green candlestick. The candlelight dimly lit the room. A beamed ceiling sloped towards the dormer window. In a saucer with a little water one of Price's nightlights on the chest of drawers created a semblance of light, company in the dark. Outside in the yard a cow mooed for her calf, an owl hooted 'Tu wit tu woo' by the barn, and I was asleep.

Not long after this a virulent flu epidemic struck England – said to have returned with soldiers from France. Our family, as many others, was laid low. The four bedrooms rang with coughs and sneezes, shivers and sweats. Dad alone remained on his feet. He sent a wire to Auntie Polly who lived with Uncle Job in a cottage near Beckford Inn, Brookside. She was to arrive on the 8.50 train. Little George Earles, under cowman, met her with Flower and the dray. He was collecting the milk churns from Fullers of Birmingham.

Auntie Polly, stout like all the family, over-fed, with rosy cheeks, put her foot on the hub of the dray wheel. George with tight reins on the young mare sat on a corn sack in front. Auntie almost made it, but halfway between the station yard and the prepared seat of hay on the dray bed she fell, broke her arm, and had to return home on the 9.40 train. George arrived without the willing nurse and Dad coped with my two grandparents, Mother, us two boys and the baby girl.

It wasn't long before Mother was up and about doling out the doctor's medicine, rubbing my chest and back with camphorated oil. From my bedroom window I could see the great green churchyard yew tree, the black naked beech trees, and could distinguish faces formed by the gnarled mossy cider apple tree in the orchard.

Ponto the odd job man wheeled a four-wheeled carriage, a miniature market gardener's dray, up the village from Beckford. Dad said it was the bier, which puzzled me even more as I saw no barrel. Then I understood that Stocky the gravedigger had been busy burying the victims of the flu plague.

What concoctions we swallowed morning, noon and night, apart from the doctor's medicine – linseed and liquorice, onion gruel, then the final dose when I was up, ipecacuanha wine, which took mucous off the chest and caused the vomiting to clear everything from the stomach. Nightly Dad took a shovel full of hot embers from the fire and poured carbolic acid on them, blowing the smoke like incense around all the rooms. It was reckoned to kill all germs. The nightly smoke screen was ritualistic. No one ever smiled.

One morning Grandma told Mother that Grandad had had a relapse and pneumonia had developed. The doctor came. Hot linseed poultices were taken regularly to his room. There was talk

Grandad's workshop

of a crisis when his temperature would reach a maximum. I wasn't allowed to see him struggling for breath in the big bedroom under the yew tree. Sunday morning Mother told me, 'Grandad's gone to live with Jesus.'

'No,' I said, 'he hasn't finished making my wheelbarrow. I don't like Jesus.'

Mother replied, 'Now you mustn't say that. Grandad wanted to go.'

I thought of the wheelbarrow and how my champion would be with me no more. I thought of when Dad smacked my bottom for having what Mother said was an accident, eating plums all afternoon under the Pershore tree. After Mother had replaced my thin green knickers Dad smacked me with his hand. Grandad had said, 'Not too hard, Tom, his knickers be very thin.' There would be no more trips to Wet Furrow to pick mushrooms for breakfast.

THE PRAYER ROOM

Stanley Farm, where I lived as a boy in the twenties, took its name from Jim Stanley, a previous owner. The bedroom where I slept with my brother was on the left hand side of the old oak staircase, a staircase which divided at a little landing. There were two bedrooms to the left of the landing and three to the right. On the left before we reached our bedroom door a great, wide, oak-studded door remained permanently bolted. This opened up to a long narrow cell-like apartment without a window. Inside the whitewashed walls flaked their limewash and the wide elm floorboards creaked. An eerie place which smelt of age and damp.

I never entered this compartment, known as the 'Prayer Room', without our dog Rip, for it harboured rats, mice and cobwebs, and bats hung from the timbered ceiling. It had been the refuge of folk of years ago who didn't conform to the established religion of the day: Roman Catholics, Nonconformists, Quakers and the like. By the light of rush lamps fuelled by mutton fat, men and women had worshipped secretly.

The only things left in this glory hole were a few old broken chairs, yellowed books on agriculture, damp, worn out counterpanes. Behind the great oaken door a wooden bar could be fixed between a giant blacksmith-made staple on one door post and half a staple on the other door post which was known as the 'clapper'. It was a good hiding place for us boys when we played hide-and-seek with friends from the town. We would take a candle in there and Rip the dog to keep us safe from the rats. There were rat holes along the outside wall through the wattle and daub panels between the beams. On windy days the draught from these honeycombed passages would make our candle flicker, casting shadows.

Whitewashing and wallpapering was an important part of spring cleaning of the old house, but the Prayer Room was never touched. Here the white was yellowed with age, the spiders' gossamer webs festooned from the gnarled and bent beams like very fine lace curtains.

Mother didn't like us playing in there – she said it could be a harbour for disease, but Dad made a special point when the flu epidemic swept the countryside of taking his shovel of live coals and pouring on the carbolic acid from the blue bottle marked poison and fumigating the Prayer Room.

The bent timbers both sides of the staircase had holes drilled in the wood; some said they were old ships' timbers which had been brought up the Severn to Tewkesbury. The holes had been neatly plugged in the timbers and the whole lot was limewashed over indoors, but outside the black and white half-timbered walls made patterns, squares, rectangles, triangles, of whitewashed work in between the black woodwork.

When Jack Hunting repaired a panel I saw the craft of the plasterer exposed. The rendered oak laths held the mud, lime and sand together to form wattle-and-daub; it looked handsome from the outside but where the rats had their runs in the hollow walls, the shells of walnuts and hazel nuts left tell-tale evidence of their habits. They even stole soap from the back kitchen and took it along their runs to the Prayer Room. Rats favoured Lifeboy soap but weren't particular. A straw hat of mine was missing from the back bedroom and found in one of the rat runs between the wattle-and-daub walls of the Prayer Room.

In summer time the rats lived out in the fields in the rickyard but when winter became severe they came in hordes to the warmth of the barns and our farmhouse. Dad fought a losing battle with them, putting Rodine poison on bread for them. It smoked as the phosphorus was spread like fish paste on bread laced with margarine and sugar. I wondered whether the rats had interfered with the men of prayer as they hid away from the Establishment.

Just below the Prayer Room door and below the landing one of the treads on the staircase was an inch or so shallower than all the rest: an ingenious idea. Having lived in the house all my life, it was second nature when going to bed to take this smaller step with candle in one hand and the other hand on the banister. The smaller step was to deceive intruders. If by any chance someone broke into the house and came up the stairs in the dark they would miss their footing at the smaller step, and wake up the household. But with a barred door, and great iron locks on the doors with keys like the keys of a church, an intruder was unlikely. The big keys for some reason were called 'the blacksmith's daughter'.

THE BACK KITCHEN, WASH HOUSE AND COAL HOUSE

Along an L-shaped stone-slab floored hall known as the passage, a wide door led to our back kitchen. The passage had blue coloured walls – walls painted with lime wash made by slaking quick lime in water to make a whitewash. This was coloured with Reckitt's Blue powder. It looked passable when first applied, but, having no oil in the mix, it flaked, so every day Mrs Vale with dustpan and brush swept up the blue flakes off the stone slabbed floor.

Mrs Vale's workplace was here in the back kitchen. A big iron range stood under the broad chimney piece. A sway – a sort of iron arm – swung from the black fire back; a chain from this swinging arm supported pot hooks, which were hung into the chosen link on the chain according to how near the iron kettle or the iron pots had to be to the roaring fire below.

Mrs Vale boiled iron pots of water for scrubbing the paved floor, the hearth. She boiled water to make mashes of potatoes (potatoes cooked by Dad in the wash house), oatmeal sharps (a by-product of wheat) for the barn door fowls. She mixed it with a wooden spoon and sprinkled Karswood spice to make them lay more eggs in winter. The smell of Karswood spice and the mash was almost appetising on winter days. Karswood spice contained, among other things, ground up insects, a magic addition to the mixture.

In the far corner of the back kitchen, past a scrubbed white kitchen table where Mrs Vale ate her lunch of bread and cheese and a great mug of cocoa, a big old corner cupboard was full of all the mystery of early veterinary science: bottles of linseed oil; turpentine for drenching cattle, horses and sheep; Pettifer's Mixture, that wonder drug for ailing sheep, sheep with red water worms, hoven or bloat. A long necked wine bottle was used to pour these mixtures down the throats of animals. Here on the shelves were all the cure-alls of the day, capsules of carbon tetrachloride for liver fluke in sheep, powders for white scour or diarrhoea in calves, known as puff hoo powders; aqua fortis, pronounced by Shepherd Tidmarsh as 'Haccle Fartis', used to burn off the diseased foot rot in sheep; bottles of Jeyes fluid to be diluted into maggot water to kill the maggots hatched from the fly blows of the blue arsed fly in the sheep's fleeces on hot sultry summer days; alum for sore shoulders on horses; Cataline for garget or mastitis in milk cows; Stockholm tar, an archaic ointment used to heal wounds on sheep made by the maggots or 'gentles', as the shepherd called them; Pettifer's green oils to lubricate and be antiseptic to ease a difficult case of lambing when the shepherd drew a lamb wrongly presented from the womb.

The corner cupboard reached from the stone flagged floor to the beamed ceiling and the poisons were on the top shelf – Cooper's sheep dip containing arsenic for dipping the sheep, and potassium cyanide for taking wasps' nests. A hollowed-out cow's horn, a drenching horn, was rarely used, a long necked wine bottle being preferred. Tom the cowman, Ralph the carter, and Alf the shepherd had access to all these remedies through the back door.

The vet from the town rarely came, for these men coped with most ailments from this department in Mrs Vale's back kitchen where everything was at hand except a proprang. If a cow was unfortunate enough to get a piece of mangold stuck in her gullet, I fetched the proprang from a neighbouring farmer known as 'Laughing Tom'. A proprang is a flexible tube of a kind of bamboo covered with leather, with a lead weight at one end. One man would hold the cow's mouth open while Tom the cowman gently pushed the end with the lead weight down the cow's gullet and dislodged the piece of mangold root. It usually worked.

Under the window in Mrs Vale's back kitchen was a miniature garden of white geraniums which was tended and watered by her on the window ledge. They seemed to be for ever in bloom. On a shelf by the side an interesting weather barometer told her something, but merely puzzled me. A glass jar with water inside had a glass bulb with a long glass pipe standing in the water. The bulb was like a big electric light bulb. According to the weather, the water rose and fell in the bulb. No doubt Mrs Vale knew how to read it. I never did.

Through a passageway and a glass door to the right was the house; a cold place, except on wash days (always Mondays), when the copper boiler, fuelled by wood, slack coal, old boots and shoes, boiled the washing under a wooden lid. There were two coppers or furnaces in the wash house; the larger of the two had been for brewing beer but Dad used it to boil potatoes for the pig. A set of shelves held washing soda and hard Windsor soap, which came in lengths of one foot six, the bars of soap divided by a deep groove. When a new bar was needed it was separated from the long bar by twisting it. Carbolic soap came in individual bars. Other shelves were loaded with packets of Hutson's soap powder, Reckitt's blue, Robin starch, Zebra black lead grate polish and Karswood spice.

On wash days the wash house was full of steam as the copper gurgled its contents to the boil and Mrs Vale fished out the washing into a dolly tub. The dolly, a wooden handled tool with a copper plunger-like head, was used to agitate the clothes in rinsing water. The big brown salt-glazed sink acted as a water-filled working top where the shirt collars were scrubbed. Some garments had several journeys from the tub to the sink until rinsed free from soap and the inevitable Reckitt's blue used to give the whites that special brightness. A big iron-framed mangle with wooden rollers turned by a wooden handle squeezed most of the water from the washing before it blew on the long line in the garden like the sails of a ship, held safe by gypsy-made clothes pegs.

When Dad had a boil up in the other copper for the pig, he put a sack of small potatoes in the water where they boiled until they were soft enough to mash with a wooden rammer in half a small cider barrel. The smell was quite appetizing and I used a pointed nut stick to prod into a cooked potato then ate it with a little salt.

Through a door with a wooden latch was our coal house. Every winter Dad shared ten tons of coal with Mr Bailey, his partner. Ralph hauled our five tons in a muck cart from the station siding and carried it through another outside door from the cattle yard to the coal house: a big room open to the roof rafters where the coal and firewood were stored for the winter. The coal shone in the candlelight in the dark place. Massive lumps from Cannock

Boiling washing

17

Chase pits, some like black diamond gate posts. It was here that I learnt to break the coal into smaller lumps for the farmhouse fire with a coal hammer, following the grain and hitting the lumps. I was fascinated to see ancient leaves of trees patterned in the coal, leaves maybe millions of years old.

Against the wall was a stack of faggots of kindling wood neatly tied with wire like brown sheaves, of withy ash and prunings from apple trees; nightly I used the chopping block and hatchet by candlelight to chop the fire sticks and take them to the fireside in a wicker basket to light the fire in the living room. The first morning tea was brewed from a tin kettle which boiled over the fire sticks with the lumps of coal forming a little circle around them. Later in the day the iron kettle replaced it on the pot hooks.

THE BOTHY AND THE GHOST

Above the back kitchen and approached by some stone steps from the court was what we called the 'bothy', a room whitewashed, yet dark, open to the roof timbers. Here not so long ago the single farm chaps slept, hired hands from Evesham or Tewkesbury Mop Fair. Mop fairs were for hiring servants and farm-workers, and were so-called because domestic servants, to indicate their speciality, took a mop with them; shepherds put wool in their hatbands, and carters worse horse hair.

Ralph the carter had worked for a Mr Slatter, hired from Evesham Mop Fair, and as a boy of eleven wasn't allowed a candle to go to bed because of the risk of fire. He told me of the hard times on the land when boys were given cider sop (bread soaked in cider) for breakfast; when hired by a farmer they had to stay one year, from one Michaelmas to the next.

I knew the bothy as a place where the sheaf-like bunches of sprout seed hung drying from the timbers to be threshed out with sticks on the boarded floor when the weather was wet in winter. Sheaves of gilly flower seed saved from the gilly field dried there, waiting for the primitive threshing.

Was Stanley Farm haunted? Uncle Jim said it was and I believed him, for the whole place was what the old folk called 'unkid' or 'unkind', but the ghost I saw was gentle, a silver-like form standing on the landing then whisping away. It stood like a guardian angel.

The bothy was a good den for hide-and-seek but not cosy like the Prayer Room. One end of the floor was littered with rabbit nets, gin traps and tin trunks painted a sickly yellow. These trunks contained a few articles of mouldy clothes, knee breeches and waistcoats which no doubt were relics of the hired boys. An old polished wooden musical box now green from damp and mould produced some sort of music. It lay neglected now Dad had his phonograph and cylinder records. Sparrows in little families trespassed through a hole in the roof to feed on the sprout seed. We shot them with Tom's air gun, caught them in a net. For why I don't know, because, like wasps, if you kill one, another one takes its place.

In Uncle Jim's boyhood Stanley Farm housed Squire Baldwyn's farm bailiff, a Somersetshire man whose speech to the farm men on the Gloucestershire/Worcestershire borders was as foreign as Chinese. When he referred to a hay rick as 'thick mow', Blenheim Allen, the cowman of 1885, looked at him and asked, 'What dost thee myun, Master Short?' Uncle said it took Master Short some time every morning to give the orders to the men, partly I suspect because they didn't take to a foreigner coming there to tell them what to do or how to do it.

Blenheim Allen told Uncle Jim that as long as he had known, and his grandfather before him, the quarter of an acre past the barn where the corn ricks were built on the old staddle stones was known simply as the rickyard. 'Now,' to quote Blenheim, 'Master Short'ull call it the Barton.' Whether it was the ghost or the rats, Master Short didn't stay long. But, as Uncle Jim used to say, 'Squire Baldwyn was a bit more than eccentric.' He kept rheumaticky old men working, coming to work on two sticks, while young strong men like Uncle Jim had the same wage.

When Mr Short left, Stanley farmhouse remained empty for years, a haunt for rats, barn owls, wild cats, a night's rest for tinkers, hurdy gurdy men, Russians and dancing bears, German bands and all the squatters of the late nineteenth century. Old Squire Baldwyn let Stanley Farm fall into disrepair, and the thatch blew off the stable and the bothy. Mr Collins bought the farm on the squire's death and rented it to Charles Slatter: a good man according to Uncle Jim, who killed a pig for his men every few weeks and kept a good herd of Shorthorn cows. One thing Charles Slatter did which perpetuates his memory. He planted horse radish in the garden and despite everything it remains there today.

Sam Eaton followed him, a hunting man who walked a couple of fox hound puppies. I believe this dog-and-stick farmer got the most part of his living from the turkeys his wife reared in the rickyard. (A 'dog-and-stick' farmer is a higgler, a trader who buys and sells stock.) Dad came to the farm as tenant in 1911, married Mother in 1913 when he could afford to; I first saw the light of day, delivered by Mrs Cotton who beat the horse-and-trap-driven nurse by half an hour, in April 1915.

Here our family lived, Chapel and teetotal, sabbath keeping and puritanical. Dad signed the Pledge, never to drink, taste, nor touch alcohol, in 1894 when Mr Nobbs, a missioner, came to the old chapel. The only cider the men had was from Sam Eaton's barrels which he still kept in the old thatched barn. Jack Hunting bored holes in the full barrels when it was fit to drink. He bored holes with a nail paster (or gimlet) or a little brace and bit type of implement and Uncle Job and Ralph sucked it through wheat straws. Grandma made homemade wine from oranges, elderberries and plums, believing in St Paul's words, 'When you are old drink no longer water but take a little wine for the stomach's sake.'

SUNDAY

Apart from Sunday School I liked the old-time sabbaths in the village when a silence which could be felt settled like the morning dew on the little community under the hill. I didn't enjoy my first year at Sunday School for Alice, who looked after the infants at Sunday School, had fits and once she had one in class and the superintendant, a grey old gentleman gardener, put a teaspoon in her mouth to prevent her biting her tongue.

At home we breakfasted together. The trains didn't run on the branch line so George Earles, dressed in his best, collected a Consignment Note from the court window and raced Min in the float with the seventeen gallon churns of milk to Ashchurch and the mainline station for Birmingham. In a navy blue suit and black low shoes, he was a different George to weekdays when he dressed in old army jacket, breeches and puttees. Maybe George had a girl to meet those Sunday mornings. I envied him the drive to Ashchurch. He told me of racing Ted Butler from Gretton along the road past the finger post at Teddington Hands and how he held Min in the station yard when the express trains roared under the bridge.

Sunday was a different world at home. The wooden toys rested in the cupboard by the piano. After breakfast in the summer time, I sat on a stool shelling the new green peas into a colander while Dad whisked the young potatoes round in a bucket of water with two sticks. Freshly dug Sharpes Express potatoes from the garden lost their tender skins and just needed looking over, no need for scraping. A magic exercise for me to see, but Dad was magic. The magic of the carbolic acid on the live coals sending fumes to kill germs.

After dinner, with rhubarb pudding, gooseberry pudding, plum pudding or apple pudding, each in its season, we went for a walk. Sometimes Alice took us. The village all took to the open air on fine Sundays. Men looked over the crops. Ladies dressed in Sunday best paraded the lanes in flowered hats and dresses new from the sewing machine. We were allowed to pick violets and primroses. Up in Boss Close where the spring water rippled from the hill towards the brook, seven cart horses made holiday on that Holy Day. They rolled on their backs, the bright steel shoes on their hooves glistened in the sun. As we entered through the gate they whinnied a greeting, somehow knowing that the halter was not to hand and the sweaty collar was on the peg in the harness room. Little Blackbird, my blind friend with only one eye, a horse jet black with a pink nose, would take an apple from Alice's hand. I loved Blackbird. He trusted us more than the others, who gambolled and kicked free from the furrow on Sundays. Min, back with George from meeting the milk train, grazed, still sweating from her ten-mile journey, apart from her carthorse fellows of the Boss Close field.

The Sundays at home on the farm were for me the backbone of village life, hard to define, yet vital. For the poor, and there were plenty, it was a rest from the sixty odd hours of battle with the weather and the soil for little in the form of money. Men who had

The carthorses' sabbath

no stock to feed spent the afternoon in bed. What a weekly treat that was after a morning spent with neighbours assessing the merits of the cottage pigs and drinking some homemade wine. Men who brought home thirty shillings [£1.50 in today's money] and had frugal wives often put the money on the kitchen table on Friday night and left it to them to divide it. A few shillings for bread, margarine, sugar, tea, coal, rent, the Sick and Dividend Club, and one shilling for the wage earner for tobacco. Sunday tea at Stanley Farm was often a tin of Roman Gold apricots and cream, eaten off a damask white tablecloth on the mahogany table in the dining room. After tea when the washing up was over a green thick tablecloth with long tassles covered the table and Dad carried in the phonograph and a pot hamper full of cylinder records. (A 'pot' hamper was a measure: it held 40 lb. sprouts, 56 lb. apples or 72 lb. plums.) The music from the records was the imperfect reproduction of military bands, marches by Sousa and Alford, the 'Double Eagle', 'Washington Post', 'Colonel Bogey'. the record began with the nasal announcement, 'This is an Edison Bell record.'

The machinery of the phonograph fascinated me: how the governors went round, miniatures of the governors in the steam engine which did the threshing. As the motor wound down, the speed of the music faded. Sometimes a scratched record repeated over and over again as the needle bedded in candle wax kept in one groove. It was Dad's little wonder of the age, mechanical music.

At a quarter to six Dad and Mother walked to Chapel and I was left with Grandma, but on wet or snowy winter nights they stayed at home. I liked that for Grandma insisted when she was in charge on an early bedtime but Dad and Mother, not to be put out by absence from Chapel, held a little service of their own. Mother played hymn tunes at the piano. The candles at the bass and treble ends were lit and flickered on to the music. Duets of Ira D. Sankey's hymns by my parents vibrated the pink glass vases on the piano and the candlelight made the glass droppers on the ornaments glow in orange and blue colours. I loved to hear them sing 'Lead Kindly Light' to the tune 'Sandom'.

Just before bedtime when Dad said, ' 'Tis time the boys went up the wooden hill,' he sang solo. 'Now the day is over, night is drawing nigh, Shadows of the evening steal across the sky.' Then we all went on our knees, except Grandma, who if she had, might have been unable to rise again because of her weight and her age. I didn't say my prayers on those memorable Sunday nights, but Dad prayed extempore, a very moving simple prayer for his children, that they would grow up honest and God-fearing.

Feeling safe in the company of such parents, safe from the howling winter wind, the drifting snow, by candlelight I walked along the stone-slabbed hall where the draught under the back door blew the yellow flame on the candlestick and the wax dripped from the candle, forming a little mound of snowy lava until it set like a sugar candy in the tray.

Nothing at all secular had been sung on Sunday but on weeknights Mother sat at the piano after tea and sang. She had, I thought, a beautiful voice. Her songs varied from 'Keep the home fires burning', 'The last rose of summer', to 'I'll sing thee songs of Araby'. As a girl she had been in demand at concerts in Evesham and the villages. She used to tell of one dark night homeward bound from Littleton when the horse brake turned over. She was thrown out, breaking her leg, a leg which was never quite straight again. She recalled how her music teacher Miss Lombardini had tired to persuade Grandma to let Mother take up singing as a profession. Years later I understood that Grandma, a Victorian, rather stern lady, would hear none of it. Her place was tailoring the riding habits for the Orleans family when the Duke lived at Woodnorton.

BROOKSIDE

When Grandad died I was four years old; too young to understand that his apparent 'sleep' in the big bedroom would be final. Uncles and aunts appeared from far-off places. Uncle Fred cycled one hundred and fifty miles from Colchester. I learnt years later that Grandad was buried at Evesham.

A house full of mourners was no place for me, so, with brother Tom, I was whisked away to Aunt Polly's. Away from the black edged envelopes containing words of sympathy, away from the out-of-season carnation-scented wreaths. Our bedroom was taken over by grown-up folk – the ones who understood death and funerals. My brother and I arrived at Auntie Polly's in time for afternoon tea. Dad unloaded a wicker basket of spare clothes from the governess car, a basket with a little wooden peg which fastened its lid. Uncle Job worked on a farm at Great Washbourne; he wouldn't arrive home until nearly six o'clock.

'Now, Tom, you will stay to tea, and how's Lily?' Auntie had a persuasive way with Dad. He was the youngest of eleven children, spoilt a bit by his older sisters.

Dad stayed a while. Auntie Polly's kettle sang and steamed over a great coal fire in the oven grate. The table was loaded with bread and butter, homemade jam and a huge currant cake. The cosied teapot awaited the boiling water from the black iron kettle. A flowered milk jug, a crystal sugar basin stood cheek by jowl with the teapot.

We ate the bread and butter, relished the raspberry jam, then Auntie Polly's shaking hand carved the cake. I think it was half excitement at seeing Dad, who was the apple of her eye, that caused his older sister to shake, spill the tea in the saucer, and tremble as she carved the cake.

'Not too much for me, Polly.' Dad's words were ignored as Auntie Polly put a great wedge of cake onto Dad's plate. 'Um, that's a bit of good. You haven't been careful with the plums (sultanas, raisins, currants). Not like Careful Billy's currant loaves. They say he used to shoot the currants in with an air gun.'

'Oh, Tom, you remind me of our mother, you do.'

I nibbled at my cake and detected a strange flavour, but listened to Auntie who then said she made her cakes with chitterling fat. I left it on my plate and Auntie Polly said, 'Come now, Freddy, eat up, your Uncle Job will soon be home for his dinner.'

Dad left us there in the lamplight in the little parlour near where the brook sang softly over the pebbles on its way to the Avon.

Uncle Job had been a carter, lived his life with horses. Auntie Polly's parlour was like a harness room. Horse brasses, brass horse bells and martingales decorated the beam over the fireplace. Life-size pink roses stared among the green leaves of the wallpaper. On the hob reeking cabbage and fat bacon simmered. The kettle steamed and sang from the pot hooks and yet another cake tempered by chitterling fat was cooking in the oven.

Auntie Polly took a wooden railway engine and a little horse and cart from the bottom shelf of the sideboard, relics of her grown-up son Bert. We played on the rag rug. Auntie at intervals opened the black oven door with a brass knob and looked at the cake.

The whole place had a smell of garden greens, bacon and steaming potatoes, while from the back kitchen a great crock bowl of ginger beer fermented as the yeast floated on a piece of toast.

Uncle Job arrived, pushing his bike up the path to the shed in the garden. 'Joby,' Auntie said, 'we've got Tom's two boys come.' She kissed his whiskered face, the face shaved once a week, and followed him as if he were some prince into the parlour. He was her prince and he thought her a princess. This pair of rural folk, who owned their little cottage, lived like some Uncle Silas and Mrs Wiggs of the Cabbage Patch. Real products of the Vale, brothers and sisters to the oxen and sheep of the field. They lived on the things that grew around them.

'Bin threshing again today, Job?' Auntie Polly said, knocking the dust from his jacket before she hung it on a hook at the back of the door.

'Ay, Polly, and the boss bin sparing with the cider, it's getting low in the barn.'

From the hob Auntie strained the potatoes and cabbage, nipped out through the door and poured the cabbage and potato water into the pig wash tub. Uncle Job didn't eat from a plate but from a meat dish. The potatoes were piled in a barrow-like heap at the one end, then the cabbage, then the hot boiled fat bacon in rashers as thick as match boxes stood about the dish in a sea of gravy. Uncle Job, with rolled sleeves showing his leather braces, smacked his lips. I was about to witness a working man with an appetite many would envy eat a meal I'll never forget.

With a bone-handled knife and fork Uncle cut great slices of fat bacon, then while still chewing that, forkfuls followed of gravied potato and cabbage. The wooden railway engine lay ignored on the rag rug as I listened, watched, smelt the product of Auntie's cooking disappear down Uncle's throat. He paused a while, mopped the sweat from his brow, belched quietly, then, when all was finished asked, 'What's for pudding, Polly?'

Among the clutch of saucepans on the hob one had a white basin simmering inside. It was an apple pudding. Auntie fished it from its saucepan. It landed on the American clothed side table. Auntie plunged a tablespoon through its white flour pasted roof and heaped pudding and apples onto a plate. 'Custard, Polly.'

'In a second, Job.' Auntie poured custard on the pudding and passed a basin of brown sugar to her husband.

Uncle Job, eager to eat the afters, had to carefully take little spoonfuls from the outside of the plate for the pudding was like an active volcano. In a few minutes Uncle Job had completed his second course.

'Coming out in the fresh air, boys?' he suggested.

My brother Tom and I followed him to the little corrugated-iron-roofed barn. Inside a sixty gallon barrel of cider lay trammed on a thing like a low sawing horse. Its wooden tap was high enough to put a jug underneath. Uncle Job turned the tap until the quart jug was half full. He drank half a jugful standing there in the barn. He then filled the jug and paused at the pig sty where the Gloucester Old Spot bacon pig stood and looked over the door. He stroked its head lovingly and said, 'It's alright, the Missus has fed you, see you in the morning.'

Back in the parlour Uncle Job took a wooden armchair by the fire. Auntie Polly poured out three glasses of her homemade ginger beer, one for her and one each for my brother and me.

Uncle Job drank the cider from a pint mug. His face shone in the firelight. He and Auntie silently passed loving messages between them. The grandfather clock ticked; in the lamplight the flitches of bacon looked yellow on the bacon rack. Auntie's tabby cat named Tiddles purred beside me on the rag rug. The four walls of Brookside enclosed a soothing tranquillity.

Uncle Job, the *Daily Chronicle* slipped from his lap, was what Auntie called 'driving them home'. His mouth wide open, completely relaxed, he snored, the notes of his snoring changing like gears from deep bass to tenor. His snoring completely took over Brookside. Auntie Polly excused him sweetly. 'Your Uncle has had a hard day threshing, he must have a little nap. He is such a one for snoring.'

Suddenly he woke up and Auntie made us bedtime cocoa and cut slices of bread and rosemary flavoured lard for supper. I liked that. Then up the narrow semicircle of staircase to bed.

I suppose it must have been ten o'clock when Uncle and Auntie went to bed. I never heard them but woke in the early hours. The whole house vibrated from their room. Waking my brother I called, 'The pig's got out from his sty.' I ran to the landing where Auntie met me and put her arm around me. ' 'Tis only your Uncle,' she said as she kissed me. 'He's snoring, driving them home.' After a week's stay with Auntie Polly, George Earles came to Brookside with Min the dark brown mare and the milk float. Auntie Polly loaded our cases and Tom and I sat on a hamper in the sour-milk-smelling vehicle which had taken the churns to the station. Plied with bread pudding, quenched with ginger beer, soon we were passing the old coaching inn of Beckford. Auntie Polly stood on the roadside waving and calling, 'Come and see us again soon, my dears.' The little rivulets of tears ran unashamedly down her fat, rosy cheeks.

Mother and Grandma waited our return. We had tea, bread, homemade butter and strawberry jam, then a little cake baked in the enamel dish by Grandma, and it was bedtime.

GAMES AND TOYS

I was twelve years old when Jack Hunting the carpenter gave me a catapult, a forked nut stick ready for the elastic to be fixed, and made for me my first instrument for field sports. 'Now bring me some catty elastic from Evesham and I'll make a catapult as good as any in the parish,' he said. At Coombs' shop next to the Gentleman's Club, Mr Coombs supplied the likes of me with catapult elastic, pea shooters, tops, pistols and caps and composition cricket balls.

With waxed thread Jack bound a length of elastic to the top of each fork of the stick. He cut an old kid glove and made a holder for the pebble, fixed it in the middle of the elastic, then gave me the homemade weapon.

There was something suspect about owning a catapult. It was questionable whether they were legal. Possessing one made me feel like having a rifle without a permit. PC Smith had confiscated catapults from some of the village boys for aiming at telephone insulators. I had five hundred acres of our land to roam and the variety of targets, live and otherwise, were legion.

Frank had a catty and was a good shot at rabbits or birds. I went with him to the brook and collected small pebbles for ammunition, then we found a heap of discarded ball bearings in the barn which were ideal. Cocoa cans placed on the rickyard wall were good practice targets, but we were thirsty to kill, and my first victim was a half-grown rabbit at ten yards. We aimed wildly at the rooks as they stole our walnuts from the rickyard trees, but they were too cunning.

Catapults were just one of the simple weapons we used to have a pot at some unsuspecting live target. Not very accurate, but good fun, were the slings we made from binder twine and old gloves. David did slay Goliath in this way, but I was no marksman with a sling.

Then one birthday I was given a King air rifle. I shot packets of lead slugs at the birds until I had more dead sparrows than the cats could pluck and eat. Then I shot field fares or velts as they gorged themselves off the crab apples in early winter. I got Mother to make a field fare pie, and felt that the housekeeping was being helped by my endeavours. The King air gun would kill a rabbit at twelve yards if the pellet hit the head. The shooting of wild life was inbred in country boys in the 'twenties – there was so much around.

Bows and arrows were hardly the thing. Our bows made of yew, and arrows of nut sticks, were used for practising. The primitive pop guns amused me – another little toy Jack showed me how to make. Taking an elderberry stick about one and a half inches in diameter and extracting the pith with a poker, or better still a brace and bit, he was left with a hollow tube a foot long – the barrel. A ramrod of nut wood pared down to go into the barrel fitting like a piston in a cylinder had a thick handle at the end to use as a plunger. I stuffed the barrel with the pith of the elder boughs and used the pop gun like a bicycle pump. It was surprising how far the pith ammunition would travel.

But the air gun was favoured by me as a secret weapon; I would creep up behind some unsuspecting sparrow in the yard. When I ran out of lead slugs I found grains of wheat could be alternative ammunition, but inaccurate and not so deadly as lead.

In March when the wind dried the untarred village street, causing eddies of Cotswold stone dust to cling to the grass verges and the hedges, we played tops. Mr Coombs had two sorts: Fliers and Dutchmen. The Fliers were long in the shank and painted with blue and white stripes. We chalked the flat tops of our toys with all the colours of the rainbow so that when they did spin and fly they were as pretty as butterflies. The girls favoured the squat round Dutchmen. The Dutchmen wouldn't carry so far in the air when whipped as the Fliers, but were more stable, easier to start. In Evesham Market Place where the road was leveller than our village, I played at tops with Billy Lunn every dinner time. There was ample space and no shop windows to break.

To everything there is a season, we read in Ecclesiastes. This applied to simple games. Hoops were the craze in February, tops in March, bird-nesting in April, and so on, with marbles and hopscotch taking their turns. Who ruled the child's sporting calender was a mystery. It was as if some unseen hand decreed when we should discard one game for another.

I was fortunate with a hoop, for plenty of iron drill rims lay in the rickyard. They made ideal hoops, while the girls had wooden hoops bought from Mr Coombs.

One birthday, I was even more fortunate to have as a present a real leather cased football laced up with leather laces like Dad's working boots. I fondled it like a girl with a doll. It was so beautiful, made up of sections of leather, tan coloured as the coat of a hare off the hill.

On the grassy banks of Holcomb Nap older boys made sledges out of the staves (curved wooden strips) and hoops of cider barrels. On hot summer days when the wiry grass crackled and almost talked in the heat, we sledged down this Cresta Run from top to bottom, a primitive ski slope.

Tip cat was dangerous, both to passers-by in the road and to windows. A tip cat was simple to make by sharpening a peg at both ends, a piece of straight ash about nine inches long. With a blow from a nut stick at either end the tip cat would fly waist high then with another whack the missile could be sent flying through the air, twenty yards or more. Hours were spent making simple toys and playing simple games, with a pocket knife as the only tool.

On Armistice days when we trooped under the Abbey Tower at Evesham, the remaining relic of the Abbey, then walked to the bronze soldier war memorial, hatless, my eyes were diverted to that great tank which had lumbered like a tired horse through the fields of Flanders. A monstrous robot on tracks which the old soldiers said would cross ditches and break through hedges armed with guns. It lay there like a sleeping tortoise, grey and ugly among the flowers and shrubs overlooking the peaceful Avon River.

We made a miniature tank from one of Mother's spent cotton reels. With a penknife I cut deep grooves in the edges of the reel and nailed a tin-tack near the hole where the reel had fitted on the sewing machine. By threading a rubber band or an elastic band through the hole and fastening one end to the tin-tack and slipping the other through a short pencil, and winding it up, my tank was ready for action. It would crawl over the kitchen table and mount obstacles such as match boxes until the elastic motor ran down. My brother Tom and I would have mock battles with tanks and put lead soldiers in strategic points to be overrun by this simple homemade toy. Plastic toys were unheard of and clockwork ones rare in the village.

Then one Christmas Tom had a real steam engine fired by a spirit lamp and when the steam was up it was a replica of Joe North's threshing machine engine from Winchcombe. It even had a whistle. That to me was wonderful beyond words.

Jack Hunting the carpenter's words were valid in those days. 'A knife, a shilling and a piece of string, and you can cut, tie and buy.'

Simple pleasures like tanks and lead soldiers took up hours by the fireside, but the cruel instinct common in all boys in the farmyard seemed innocent to me, yet a feeling of shame came later. The sparrows' nests in the thatched roof of the Bull Pen were raided incessantly by me and Frank. We took the multi-coloured eggs of the house sparrow and swapped them at school, pierced at both ends with a pin and blown. The chaff and corn in the barn was alive with sparrows which our elders the farmers knew as enemies of the cornfields and the corn ricks. When the fledgelings were almost fit to fly we made them swim in the horse trough and unashamedly drowned them.

COUNTY CLOTHES

In the 'twenties there was an evident apartheid between town and country. This difference became very plain to me at the age of thirteen. Being what was known as a 'hobbledehoy', neither a man nor a boy, is for everyone a dramatic experience. I became shy in the company of girls and self-conscious on Sundays when as a farmer's son I was dressed in dandified clothes so alien from the knockabout gear of the farm. This was partly the influence of my headmaster who impressed on parents how his pupils should dress on Sundays.

At Lloyds, the shop in Evesham, the fitting out of Sunday best was, to put it mildly, a frightening experience: black jacket in good cloth with waistcoat to match, grey pin-striped trousers, a white shirt with a most uncomfortable starched collar, and a black-and-white tie. I went through contortions to fix the collar to the back stud, restricted like a dog by a fourteen and a half inch collar. Walking up Ashton village that first morning to the chapel was like running the gauntlet between my short-trousered soberly dressed friends.

At school Christmas parties that was different, for I was a young man of the town dressed as what Shepherd Tidmarsh called a 'townie'. On Saturdays and school holidays the old jersey, blazer and short trousers had been for walking the fields among the stock with Dad, or along with Ralph and the horses, Tom and the cows, or the shepherd in the sheep fields.

On Saturday outings to Gloucester Market Dad wore breeches and pigskin gaiters and brown, lightly nailed boots; a footwear midway between his working hobnails and his Sunday light black boots which Mr Bailey his partner called 'tea drinkers.'

'I'm going to get Fred some market clothes like you, Tom,' Mother said one autumn day when we were shopping in Evesham. At Huin's, Mother's favourite shoe shop, she bought me a pair of brown, lightly nailed boots like Dad's and a pair of pigskin gaiters or leggings. The row of buttons were like mother-of-pearl, yellow and glazed. When the gaiters had been worn a few times, I got the knack with the buttonhook of fishing the button through the buttonhole.

Old fashions die hard in a village. Doctor Roberson, perhaps the last of the gentry apart from Mr John Baldwyn, still wore frock coats with cloth-covered buttons and box hats, top hats in miniature. It was noticeable however that the younger men of the village began to ape the townsmen. Drainpipe trousers, a little on the short side, showing fancy patterns on their socks, known as clocks, didn't stay for long for Sunday gear. They were superseded by wide Oxford bags in silver grey. Mr Bettridge advertised these in the local journal. I remember one of his adverts. 'Having bought trousers in bulk, I can now offer them at slaughter prices.'

Harry Bettridge and his Bon Marché was a great friend to the thirty shilling a week labourer of the land, for if a couple of his famous Oxford shirts were purchased he'd throw in a pair of socks or a flat pancake cap as a bonus. So the difference between the countryman's clothes and that of what the shepherd called the townie was apparent to me.

Dad decided that if and when I started work in earnest, that to be warm and dry among the crops, the dripping sprout leaves and the dew drenched mangolds, he should rig me out in the right way. So to West's we went one Saturday morning where he bought me a pair of Bedford cord breeches and a grey tweed jacket complete with an inside poacher's pocket big enough to hold a rabbit.

Then to that famous boot emporium, Messrs Wyld's, where the well-known Plough and Harrow brand of boots were uniform among the workers of the land. These boots were heavy with two rows of hobnails forming an oblong track around the edge of the sole and a horse shoe of steel to cover the heel. It was like shoeing a horse at Tom Higgins blacksmith's shop to fit my tender feet into Plough and Harrow boots.

A pair of pigskin leggings with a row of buttons took what seemed minutes to put on above the boots. Dad smiled and said, ' 'Tis no good if he has to use a buttonhook and put those on, he will never be ready for work in the morning.' So the conventional black leather leggings with a strap at the top and a short length of fastening like clock springs, which slid into a metal slot at the bottom, were decided upon.

This outfit proved really practical on the Midland clay when I was used to it. Wyld's manager threw in a tin of Carr's dubbin, an extra pair of leather laces and some insole socks. I looked forward to being conventional, the working clothes would not be as conspicuous among the farming folk as the black coat, pin stripes and starched collar which had brought the village a little nearer to Eton.

That afternoon, rabbiting with Dad and his partner Mr Bailey educated my feet in the first lesson of hobnails. Coming down

Bredon Hill in the twilight my feet felt as if they were shod with lead, and I lagged, carrying the bag of rabbits. That night when the laces were undone, with the ease of the carpet slippers, bed came none too soon.

Sunday morning, still conscious of the dandy black and pinstripe, my new low shoes from Huin's with patent leather toe caps were easy on my blistered feet. 'You'll have to break those boots in a bit at a time, Fred. It's like breaking in a horse, and then you will be like the rest of us. Oh, they call us clod hoppers, but that's about it on the land,' Dad said.

So I dubbined them and softened the leather, then went to the stable where Ralph gave me neatsfoot oil to soften them further. They were waterproof in the days when Wellington boots were rare and despised by the old hands of the farm. I remember testing their waterproof quality by standing in four inches of water in the horse trough, my feet as dry as a bone. There were two tongues in Plough and Harrow brand, a little tongue from the toe, then another which covered the whole of the front of the foot under those leather laces.

Wearing hobnails gave the feeling of being one of the men, for after dark I could make sparks fly on the road like the shepherd as he scuffed his boots clean from the sheep barn to his home at Lilac Cottage. Soon the boots were broken and appreciated by feet, warm and dry in all weather; leather leggings or gaiters protected legs in dew drenched grass or the clinging clay of the plough land. Wet weather, before the Wellington boot came to the village, had to be combated. There were various ways of keeping the legs and feet dry. Leggings or gaiters did help above the dubbined or sometimes cart-greased hobnailed boots. Puttees from the '14 war were warm and fairly weather-proof. In the sprout fields when the leaves were soaking wet potato sacks tied on with binder twine were wrapped round the legs, and two and a quarter hundredweight corn sacks put over the shoulders and tied around the neck would keep out a fair amount of rain. What a benefit the Wellington boots were and oilskin overcoats. I do remember Mr Bailey, Dad's partner, taking the men out to the fields from the barn on wet days. 'We shan't melt, we aren't made of sugar,' was one of his stock sayings.

In summer the picture of the hayfields was like a Bruegel. A variety of straw hats, battered panamas, kept off the sun and were

Bonnets and cider among the hay

a barrier against the hay seeds for the hay pitchers, more so when the men with hobnailed boots on the waggon wheel hub tightened the waggon rope when the load was ready for hauling from the fields. However hot the weather was, the haymakers wore their waistcoats while under their Oxford shirts flannel undershirts mopped up the sweat. To discard an undershirt was, I was told, just asking for a chill. I never saw a bared chest in the hay or harvest field and the only hatless man I remember was Bertie Richardson, the driver of the steam threshing tackle. His bald head was bronzed winter and summer and he and Uncle George used to go shopping together at Evesham on Saturday nights, each carrying a basket which held something between a peck and a bushel.

The village women worked in the fields in summer with their pleated bonnets all white, with a generous piece of material over the nape of the neck to keep off the sun. They wore aprons made of hurden, a kind of sacking, but on Sundays some of their hats trimmed over and over again on the same usually black straw frame were like baskets of summer fruit.

CHAPTER TWO

Farm Animals

PIGS

Careful Billy the Beckford baker kept a few Large White sows which he crossed with a Large Black boar. The litters were reared on the sows until they were eight weeks old, then sold to the cottagers in the Bredon Hill villages. His young store pigs, or weaners, were what was known as 'sheeted pigs'. On a white background the inheritance of the boar had left patterns of a bluish black, like a map of the world. The older folk who had fattened pigs all their lives liked the sheeted pig, a half breed, which grew fat and long. Careful Billy supplied their food – the sharps or middlings, the barley meal – and delivered it from his dray on his bread round. No one except Careful Billy made money from pigs. He was in business as a breeder.

We fattened two pigs as a rule and, like the cottagers, bought our weaners from Careful Billy. On the edge of one village in the Vale a small herd of sows in an old orchard used to scrump Warners King apples, thriving on them and a little meal. These were Gloucester Old Spot pigs, known as orchard pigs, extremely hardy, preferring to live out of doors. They grew a rough white coat in winter with spots of black bigger than half-crowns [coin equivalent to 12½p in today's money]. They were useful animals, living on roughage. Dad fattened one one year but said the rind, what he called the 'sward', was thick and hard, and really the Gloucester Old Spot wasn't happy couped up in a sty. It's a ranging pig.

In the 1920s every cottager kept a pig: their needs were one or two pigs to fatten for bacon so that from October until the following October flitches of bacon hung on the kitchen walls or on bacon racks, an insurance, with potatoes, of food. Real self-sufficiency. Some with large families fattened two pigs. In the days long before the council collected the garbage with a dust cart all the household scraps found their way into the pig wash barrel. This stood by the back door of each cottage near a soft water butt. Potato peelings, parsnips, half-rotten apples, washing up water left over from dinner plates, water the vegetables were cooked in, sour milk, all found their way into the pig swill. It fermented and formed a scum on top of the wash and when ladled out into a bucket to be mixed with sharps or middlings, barley meal, etc., the smell was beyond description, but the pigs lapped it up in

Gloucester Old Spots and windfall apples

their troughs and thrived. A number of these pigs were Gloucester Old Spots, but there was a breed known as the Cottagers Pig, a hardy type of Large White.

On Sunday mornings men of the land swopped ideas on feeding, assessed the weight of their pigs. Their wives gave the pigs cabbage from the garden at midday and a little heap of slack coal to keep them in condition. Cottagers' pigs were a part of the family, so different from the commercial production by the farmers. Farm workers' wives became attached to the grunting from the sty so some went out for the day to town when the pig killer came. One neighbouring farmer kept some sows, he also kept sheep on the hill. When he lost a ewe through lambing he skinned it then dragged it into the yard. His sows ate it and saved him the trouble of burial (illegal of course today). He did have trouble when he killed one pig for bacon for the house: having been fed liberally on fish meal, the bacon was uneatable, smelling of fish.

Nearly every village had a Pig Club, a sort of Sick and Dividend Club for pigs, so that if someone's pig died he was compensated out of the club fund.

Joe Whittle was the pigkiller, he came to us as he came to the cottages. One frosty morning, holding tight to Grandad's hand, I stood and witnessed the kind of sacrificial execution in the yard. The squeals as the pig was coaxed backwards from the sty, then two strong men with cord trousers and hobnailed boots held it on the bench. Joe put in the knife. Its squealing stopped, it lay motionless on a bed of straw. Then Joe lit the straw, burning it until every bristle was gone. Joe took a broom and swept the burnt hair and straw from the carcass. The frosty air was scented by a burnt offering of bristle.

Buckets of hot water bathed it, Joe scrubbed it until its blackened body was as white as the hoar frost in the yard. The men hung it on a beam in the back kitchen and the hidden secrets of its inside were revealed steaming. Mother and Grandma scurried in and out of the kitchen with big willow pattern dishes of liver, heart, chitterlings.

Joe, after he had put a nut stick as a spreader, leaving its clean empty belly to cool in the winter air, came into the house place where Dad had a hooped frying pan suspended on the pot, hooked over the fire, larded ready to receive a portion of the warm liver for Joe's lunch. Joe sat up at the table and ate the liver with the top of one of Percy Smith's cottage loaves, using Dad's own bone-handled knife and fork. He ate the meal as if he had never had liver before, yet it was the custom of generations that the pig killer was entitled to the first meal of liver warm from the pig.

MILK COWS

A picture in the Brookside hams (pastures near to the river) in early summer was one of cows grazing on the dew drenched grass until the sun and heat drove them to the shade of the withy trees; the yellow of buttercup, of cowslips, mingled with the old ley, pasture which hadn't felt the plough share since the Crimean War, full of herbs, trefoil, vetches, clover.

The Shorthorn cows were mostly dark red with a few roans; no black-and-white Friesians had arrived. Every year the Shorthorn cows gave us a half-bred Hereford calf from Samson the bull. These calves, with calves bought in, were reared on some of the second class citizens of the herd; cows with three quarters or one teat. 'Blind' was the term for a teat which gave no milk. A cow with two quarters would rear a couple of calves. These outcasts of the milking herd reared the calves which became yearlings, then at two years old were sold as fresh stores. I liked the term 'fresh stores'. It meant that they would soon be fit for beef. An animal which didn't conform and was known as a bad doer was called 'plain'.

The cream of the milking herd stood in a long line in an open shed each morning and evening, chained to a wooden manger which had a slate bottom. The chains ran through a ring on the manger and every chain had a wooden chog to act as a weight. When the cow dipped its mouth into the manger, the chog fell to the floor taking up the slack chain. These chogs were about six inches square with a hole drilled in the middle where the 'T' piece of the chain was threaded through.

Fred Randalls and George Earles milked the same cows; the cows knew their milkers. From greasy three-legged stools Fred and George squeezed the milk from the udders, five gallons a day

from Spot, but four gallons was the rule. They wore their caps back to front, greasy cow-hair covered caps, and dug their heads into the left hand flank of the cow until the cow drew her left foot back to enable the men to milk first the two front teats then the two back ones. They finished off with forefinger and thumb, what they called stripping out. The main milking was done by squeezing the teats in turn with all the fingers. Chee chaw, chee chaw, it sounded in the bucket.

As the three-gallon buckets were nearly full, the frothy milk was poured into two five gallon buckets which Fred Randalls carried from a shoulder yoke to the milk hut. Here the tank on a wooden frame was filled with luke warm milk. The luke warm milk trickled in a steady stream down over a cooler into a churn below. By that time the milk was as cold as the water which cooled it. There was a gauze strainer at the mouth of the seventeen gallon churn to catch the bits of chaff or hair which may have been in the buckets. Then it was taken to the station and put on the train for Birmingham, where Fullers collected it from New Street Station. Every week Mrs Bailey made butter in her dairy and shared it between her family and ours. Mr Bailey

Patted butter

turned the butter churn with the separated cream inside until the tell-tale flop, flop, flop meant the butter had come. Mrs Bailey worked it not into little half-pound slabs but brick-sized blocks stamped with a fancy decoration by the butter pats she used. We never made any cheese but every time a cow calved the cowman took the first milking home to make a rich beasting pudding, some called it cherry curds.

George Hunting milked sometimes on Sundays and warned me never to learn to milk, 'or else you can be a stopgap when the cowman's away.' The Shorthorn cows were mostly red apart from three or four roans and were mated to a Hereford bull named Samson and afterwards to Joker, a pure bred Hereford bull we bred from Grannie, a Hereford cow.

Cows usually were milked for nine or ten months in the year and rested for two or three months before each calving. Some were difficult to dry off before resting, but Fred Randalls had his ways, such as rationing the cow cake and milking them once a day until they were dry.

Fred Randalls was a short, stocky man. I used to watch him milking a cow in calf. He'd smile and say, 'That calf inside there is anxious to come and see us, it's kicking smartish.'

Fred on winter evenings was anxious for his cows to clear up all the hay, before, by hurricane lantern light, he drove them to the field in Didcot Ham down Gypsies Lane. 'That's it for tonight, boy,' he'd say to George Earles, 'you can get off home.'

I stayed and Fred took his tin whistle from a shelf in the milk hut and played a few tunes as we sat in the lantern light. Then the chains were unloosed from one end of the cow shed to the other. The staid old cows left quietly, ambling across the yard. The heifers strained at the chain and Fred spoke to them and patted their necks as he loosed them. They trotted down the road in front of the older cows who walked carefully along the grass verge saving their feet from the stones of the lane. The cows were kept out at night then, both winter and summer.

Fred Randalls I found to be a gentleman. I think his patience was near breaking point one Sunday when he was wearing a clean pair of corduroy breeches and one of the line of cows bespattered him with loose muck. 'Look, Fred,' he said, 'that cow has done her nast all down my clean breeches.' 'Nast' was a good description.

One morning Fred Randalls came to the back door after the morning milking. He looked grave. 'Master, the four cows in the lidded place be off their fittle (food). They foam at their mouths and their feet be sore. Oh dear, Master, they look middling.' His words struck like a knife for the old man seemed to know it was foot and mouth disease. I followed master and man across the yard. The seventeen gallon churns of milk were cooled ready for the 8.20 train to Birmingham. 'Leave the milk where it is,' Dad said to young George Earles who was ready with the float to take it to the station.

While Dad and Mr Randalls looked at the cows I peeped over the door and saw Peasbrook and Cherry snorting over their cattle cake in the manger, dribbling like babies and licking their inflamed feet. 'I'll ring Mr Hoddenot the vet. Don't turn them out to the field,' Dad said.

First of all Dad turned the little black handle on the wooden box of the extension phone and called his partner. 'Harry, you'd better come up and look at the cows. I'm just phoning Hoddenot. It looks like foot and mouth disease.'

Mr Bailey arrived and I'd never seen them look so sad, standing there with Fred Randalls. It was as if their whole world had fallen into little bits.

Mr Hoddenot was in no doubt, there were cases of foot and mouth in the Vale.

'What will happen to the cows?' I asked Mr Randalls.

'I daren't think about it, boy,' he replied.

'Now, Mr Bailey, have you any cattle in the yard at the Old Manor?'

'Yes, and the bull,' he replied.

'Wash your boots in this disinfectant and don't go near them,' were the vet's instructions.

The next day it was confirmed and I watched Mr Randalls carrying hay and water to the chog-chained milkers in their stalls. He and George Earles milked as usual but the milk remained to turn sour in the churns. Fred Smith the policeman arrived on his bike and Ministry men put buckets of Jeyes Fluid at all the gateways.

Stanley Farm was in a state of siege. The only exit for me was through the back kitchen door and here I dipped my boots in Jeyes Fluid to pass the nut bushes along the path to the privy. I'd dawdle that fifteen yard path and watch while a man from the Ministry valued the cows.

Next morning Ralph came with a load of coal from Beckford and unloaded it in the back garden behind the cowshed, then he fetched a dray load of wood faggots and dry long logs. George Earles brought a drum of paraffin from I don't know where. P C Smith stayed in our house all night keeping a watch on the exits from the yard and kipping down on the sofa in the house. A man came, armed with a humane killer, then Fred Randalls came, crying like a child, the tears making rivulets down his unshaved face and said, 'Master, can I go home? I can't stop and see this lot.'

'Yes, Fred,' Dad replied. 'I understand. We'll manage.' Fred Randalls never worked again.

Creeping silently along through the nut bushes to the little two seater earth closet I peeped through a slit window about twelve inches high and five inches wide. The men were driving Peasbrook and Cherry from their stalls through the little gate onto the half acre back garden of the farm. The privy was small, white washed, with a plastered ceiling, a tin of Keatings powder was on the covered seat, while on the wall the almanac hung from a rusty nail. A picture of a man, a shepherd with a lamb across his shoulders, walking through the snow. He carried a lantern which gave golden rays over the winter scene. Behind him walked a newly lambed ewe. Under the picture were Newman's words, 'Lead kindly light amid encircling gloom, Lead thou me on, The night is dark and I am far from home, Lead thou me on. Keep thou my feet, I do not ask to see, the distant scene, one step enough for me.'

I thought of Fred Randalls and the encircling gloom, and how he had prided himself that Spot, a cow which stood in the middle of the long shed, had given 5 gallons a day. It was going to be all over for Mr Randalls. Peasbrook, lame and looking starved after two or three days of little food, was goaded towards a spot where the fire, the unlit fire, was laid. The report from the humane killer was not loud like a twelve bore as Peasbrook fell to the ground. Cherry followed, her flanks drawn in, her hip bones showing, the result of disease and starvation. She smelt the blood, she smelt death and hesitated a moment, then she fell by Peasbrook's side.

Ralph had Turpin, the chocolate coloured gelding, in traces.

He looked wild-eyed at the dead cows as Ralph fixed a chain around Peasbrook's horns and dragged her to the laid fire. Men had been working, digging a great hole in the garden, then laying the faggots of wood, the coal ready to burn the plague, to burn the cows, Fred Randalls's cows.

Fireman Davis, who once drove the steam ploughs and lodged with Jasper Chandler the wheelwright, appeared to be in charge of the fire, helped by Jubilee Drinkwater the coalman and Joe Spires. Joe had driven a railway engine on the L.N.E.R. and travelled quite a bit. A kind man, but willing to do his bit at any unpleasant job. I believe it was his grandfather who once applied for the job as hangman at Gloucester Gaol and the name Hangman Spires stayed with him for the rest of his days.

I stayed in my hide until most of the cows were killed, but when Spot approached this kind of scaffold, I ran back to the house. It was as if the shooting of Spot, who among the others in the long shed were so far free of disease, was the last straw in the life of Fred Randalls. It seemed so pointless to me. Dad stood by policeman Smith and alone saw the passing of a herd.

Then Laughing Tom, a small farmer, came to help with the fire. He told Dad that in the old squire's time foot and mouth diseased cows would recover in time if fed on slops, bran mashes, but they became devilish poor before they recovered. He spoke of the years before slaughter was compulsory. Nineteenth-century farming.

At dusk on that fine November day the whole pyre was soaked in paraffin and the black smoke rose high above the walnut tree in Mr Nicklen's orchard. The flames licked the carcasses.

At tea I sat between Constable Smith and Dad. A tea time which lingers like a ghostly dream for hardly a word was said over the bread and butter. Butter made from our milk by Mrs Bailey. Then Dad smiled and said, 'You know Grannie, the Hereford Cow, the one Mr Randalls called the Babby's cow, it was her milk which reared you. She's down in the long Dewrest with other cows, dry and in calf. They won't kill Grannie.' I had watched her being milked so many times. Mr Randalls always left her to last for her big tits were loath to give the milk down. I pictured Fred Randalls wresting the milk from her and heard him say, 'When I teach you to milk it won't be on Grannie, it's like getting blood from a stone.'

Dad handed me a milk can and a lantern and asked me to fetch a can of milk from Mr Clements. 'And before you go, dip your shoes in the disinfectant. I wouldn't like Hughie's cows to catch foot and mouth.'

I walked quickly past the garden where the fire illuminated the apple trees. Mr Clements filled my can and said, 'How is your Dad taking it, Fred? I'm very fond of Tom, your Dad. You tell him that he can have all the milk you need.'

I replied, ' 'Tis Mr Randalls I am sorry for. He's a good man, Mr Clements.'

As the school windows shone in the light of my lantern, I passed the Star Inn where the lantern lit sign gently squeaked in the breeze. A breeze from the Cotswold Edge which brought with it the pungent stench of burnt flesh. Around the fire men were working with forks, their eerie figures in the smoke could be recognized by the firelight. Two men would throw another log of wood onto the flames as Fireman Davis was tossing great lumps of coal from a heap nearby. The scene was one of sacrifice. A costly sacrifice of years of breeding of Shorthorn milkers. Constable Smith stood by, his helmet picked him out from the men tending the fire.

As I lay tossing in bed that night I heard the crackle of the fire and that memorable smell of burning animals somehow came to my bedroom. Looking from the window, I saw the spooky figures of men, the firelight casting shadows to the Bramley apple tree now almost denuded of its leaves, and the shiny buttons on Policeman Smith's uniform.

At breakfast the next morning Dad and PC Smith sat in the inglenook by a fire which had burnt in the grate all night for our policeman, who had not been to bed, but had been coming and going from the garden. Percy Attwood's bullock and another one which had symptoms of disease were on the fire with the milkers. His other bullocks were driven to our yard, slaughtered and dressed by an Evesham butcher and taken in a lorry to the butcher's shop along with ten calves which had been in the barn.

The night followed the same pattern. Stoking the fire while Mother took tea and bread and cheese for the workmen.

The following morning coming down to breakfast I smelt an appetizing smell from the kitchen. The hooped frying pan hung over the fire sizzling with liver and bacon. Dad and PC Smith were just about to breakfast. 'Do you fancy some, Fred, it's liver from the calves,' Dad said.

'Yes, I really do,' I replied.

'Your brother Tom won't have any,' PC Smith said.

'Tom's like that, a bit choice,' Dad said as we relished our breakfast. 'He never likes to see the pig killed,' he added.

The fire burnt for a week and it was a fortnight later when Ralph shovelled the red ashes into a cart and spread them all over the garden and I could see little bits of bone, relics of the herd. The ashes were still hot and Ralph was afraid they might set fire to the muck cart. The siege was over, but the disinfectant smell at the doors and gateways remained.

I visited Fred Randalls many times at his thatched cottage, and the following spring he would sit under his plum tree and play his melodeon. His tunes to me on the tin whistle after milking in the cooling house were just a memory, but I persuaded him to play it in his garden. What a gentle man he was, one of nature's gentlemen. One of his daughters was courting a young smart plasterer, name of Len. Led rode a long tanked Norton motor bike and pulled all the stops out when he passed Mr Randalls's garden gate. One evening he rode by, his cap back to front, his eyes goggled. Mr Randalls turned to me and said, 'He must be going a mile a minute. He'll be the death of me.'

But no, the slaughter of a herd of cows was the death of Fred Randalls: he died a few months later, of a broken heart. I wondered where had this dreaded disease come from. Shepherd Tidmarsh said that he saw a fox among the milkers early one morning. Some said it was the starlings which fed on the asparagus bower and flew homeward to Hinton Roughs. The mystery to me at the time was that Blenheim Allen, Mr Nicklen's cowman, walked his cows from the Rails Close, behind Fred Randalls's herd, as they came up Gypsies Lane from Didcot Ham the evening of the football match the day before the cows had the disease.

STORE CATTLE

The store cattle which spent their last winter on Bredon Hill had been with us since they were calves two and a half years ago. The previous summer they grazed between the hawthorn bushes on Furze Hill. The spring water which ran from the scrub-covered bank was a constant stream until it reached a stone trough where the cattle drank. As pure as crystal and as cold as ice, the water was invaluable in summer. The shade of the hawthorn acted as a refuge from the bree flies which would torment cattle in July, so that in unshaded pastures cattle would race like thoroughbreds, losing the weight that they should have been gaining every week. When I was sent to count them every day in summer, I knew where to find them – in the shade of hawthorn and elder. They grazed at night after the sun went down.

By November the cattle were taken through the bridle gate to Spring Hill, a shelf-like plateau on Bredon. Here the grass, ungrazed in summer, was wiry and coarse. The men broadcast agricultural salt on the grassland to sweeten the pasture. The cattle wrapped their tongues around the sward, but by Christmas they needed hay as well as the cattle cake.

As yearlings the store cattle had wintered in the yard, fed on oat straw, hay, chaff, mangolds, ground oats and a little cattle cake. They stayed there until May Day before going out to grass.

Store cattle never had the best of fodder or pasture until the time when they were partly fattened for market. When the Christmas holidays came and Tom Whittle had forty cattle to feed on the top of Bredon Hill by Great Hill Barn, I helped with the foddering. Turpin, the chocolate brown gelding out of Bonnie, was kept on Spring Hill for carting the hay. Every morning after ten o'clock bait we walked up the hill, caught Turpin and hitched him in a muck cart.

Tom's rhythm with the hay knife was just poetry in motion to me. He whet the blade with what we called a rubber, a whetstone, then cut kerves of hay like thick door mats, square and firm, and rolled them from the top of the rick for me to place on the cart until it was loaded.

The forty strong store cattle, all heifers, Shorthorn Hereford Cross, stood in line under the wall waiting for breakfast. I led Turpin in a straight line across the bleak winter hill while Tom forked the fodder in heaps for the herd. A satisfying job when the ground was bone hard with frost and every wisp of hay was eaten, none trampled underfoot. In Great Hill Barn a stack of kibbled cattle cake – half linseed, half cotton – had been bagged and taken there by Ralph. Tom carried the cake to the next field through a bridle gate and put the rations in forty half nine gallon cider barrels. We opened the gate and soon the cherry red heifers had licked the last oilseed from their improvised mangers. Their coats were mossy thick and as weatherproof as they could be. The area around the barn was thick with cow pats, brown, firm from the hay and cake, fertile stuff. Tom said, 'There's no goodness in a green grass turd.'

Tom would walk through a herd of cattle on the hill, point his stick at one and say, 'Her looks a bit tucked up.' She would raise her tail and the dung would squib loose and liquid from her. Tom would examine it carefully and say, 'I'll be dalled. I just hope it yunt Johnes disease, but one thing, it yunt bubbly. If you come up on your own in the morning, just keep an eye on her.' Often it was a chill, the result of the frost on the early morning grass, but if she stood apart from the bunch we would take her home and drench her.

Before the spring sales Tom would take pride in the red and white heifers, describe them to me as well ribbed up, looking kind. Kind, usually spoken as 'kynd,' meant thriving, while unkind, sometimes referred to as 'unkid', was a beast which didn't thrive. A 'screw' was one destined for the knacker's yard.

In the early spring Ralph would chain harrow the hill and scatter the cow dung, the mole hills and leave a pattern of harrowed grass with one width laid one way and the return journey laid another, to fertilize the hill; forty strong stores would be at the Gloucester Market Spring sale to be finished by the Severnside grazers and beef fatteners.

BRUCELLOSIS

I never saw a prettier bunch of heifers than the ones Dad brought from Ireland. They were cherry red Shorthorns ready for putting to the bull. Our bull Joker was too big for heifers so I helped Tom Whittle to drive the twelve heifers to Great Washbourne and turn them up with a young Hereford bull belonging to Mr Harry Roberts.

When they came back we put them in Big Holbrook, a

meadow at Kersoe Grounds alongside the brook and the withy trees. It was my job to count the cattle every day in the holidays and Saturdays and Sundays.

When the bree fly made the cattle brevit (run round in circles) in the summer sun they would take to the shade of the bushes or stand knee deep in the brook and swish their tails. At a given signal from the leader, with tails erect, they would circle the field madly when they heard the buzz of the fly, then rush under the drooping withy trees and let the leaves brush their backs.

How good it was to go up there on the edge of night when the sun went down and they were grazing happily or very early in the morning before sunrise when the dew soaked through the leather of my boots, penetrating much more than a rainstorm.

Shade for the Herefords

The big cattle outwintered on the hill were sold in the spring for fattening at Evesham and Gloucester, warranted 'home bred, barren, right and straight and outliers'. The auctioneer said these words parrot fashion, but they were right and straight. A bunch of thirty-five had replaced them on the hill on May Day from our cattle yards. I suppose they roamed fifty acres of scrub land, rabbit holts and wiry grass. When the sun was hot the counting of thirty-five as they dodged me among the hawthorn was a bit of guesswork.

'Cattle all there, Fred?' Dad would say over midday dinner.

'Yes,' I said hopefully.

'The incalvers at Kersoe, and have you shovelled out the watering place lately?'

'Yes, Dad,' I replied.

I walked quickly around the hill and couldn't take my pony because the incalvers were the other side of the big wood and I took a short cut over the stiles. I always hindered half an hour with Arthur the gamekeeper studying the pheasant chicks and listening to his lore, the lore of game, of predators. Then I'd see

his shot or trapped vermin on a rail by his hut, a mixture of fur and feather on his gibbet. I remember seeing his twelve bore bringing down a sparrow hawk with a pheasant chick in its talons, both dead.

One day eleven heifers grazed Big Holbrook, the other beast stood looking tucked up and ill under the hedge. I saw that a rope of cleansings or after birth hung under her tail. Rushing home to Dad I told him what I'd seen and Tom Whittle and I returned to the field after dinner.

Tom said, 'Where is that other ayfer?' He always said 'ayfer'. We found her in the same place as she had been in the morning.

'Now there's a calf somewhere,' Tom said gravely. 'Hers aborted.'

'The others are alright,' I replied.

'Ah, but 'tis contagious,' he said.

The calf was found, a miniature white faced Cross Hereford about as big as a hare. The twelve heifers seemed doomed for slaughter rather than calf rearing if they aborted. Every day I went there, apprehensive, half expecting another premature birth. One by one they followed suit, casting their calves at six months in calf and never cleansing for days, weeks after calving.

Nine were put in Paris Hill Barn. Jack Hunting made a manger and I suckled a bought calf on each cow night and morning. I suppose the heifers gave about a gallon a day of this germ-loaded milk and no one saw the danger of Tom Whittle or me getting brucellosis from handling the infected animals.

There was no water in Paris Barn. Every day I carried two buckets full on a pair of yokes from Paris Gardens, a spring a quarter of a mile away up the hill. The calves when they grew older drank more water, so Ralph took a tankful up there with Flower in the dray. Soon the heifers were dry and put to the bull again, injected by the vet with S.19, a wonder drug. But next year they aborted again and went to market as barreners for about fifteen pounds a piece.

Tom said, 'Ay, them as keeps hosses be bound to have losses.'

But the thought of what might have been had the heifers gone their full time and calved naturally stuck in my mind. Foot and mouth, liver fluke in the sheep, now brucellosis. Nature was cruel.

THE SHEEP FOLD

The Great Cross Barn stood on rising ground at the foot of the hill. It had recently been thatched. The newly laid straw shone golden in early spring among the orchard of budding trees: tall Pitmaston Duchess pear trees all bursting with life in early March. Soon the whole two-acre plot would be snow white blossom.

This was Shepherd Tidmarsh's province, an exquisite private sanctuary at the very end of the farm. Inside the beams of the roof were all numbered in Roman numerals where the pegged joints held the cathedral-like structure together. The two great oaken wooden doors with heavy hinges, asped and stapled where they met, were tall enough to take a waggonload of hay. Even when the sun shone it was dark and smelt of generations of sheep.

At the one end a wooden fence with a little door fastened with a peg formed a pen for ewes and new born lambs, divided by withy hurdles into twenty ward-like compartments just big enough to take a ewe and her lambs. The open end held the ewes near to lambing and here under two lanterns they spent the nights under the shepherd's eye.

For a whole month the shepherd never went to bed, he lived in the barn. But after tea on those evenings when the days lengthened, Dad walked with me to the barn and took over from the shepherd, and Shepherd Tidmarsh walked, crook in hand, with his Collie Rosie to his cottage to spend four or five hours on his sofa. I'd sit awhile in the lantern light while Dad looked around the ewes. The red rumped ones marked by the raddle from the rams in the autumn were the first to lamb while the ones marked blue would be a few weeks later.

Some evenings in the quiet of the barn a ewe would start to bleat – more of a telltale plaintive noise than the usual baa – a signal that she had started giving birth. We would single her out and put her in one of the private wards between the hurdles, and wait. I'd sit and look at the great vaulted roof of the barn as the bats flitted around the beams; at the whole ash trees which Jack the rough carpenter had fixed where the roof dipped under the weight of the strawed roof. The shepherd had told me that Bill the local thatcher had spent so long working on the barn that he had drunk a whole hogshead of cider.

The shepherd's chancel barn

Every ewe that lambed was given a bowl of water and an armful of sainfoin hay in the wooden racks in the pen, and the afterbirth, or cleanings, was carried on a fork outside to be buried in the morning. I left Dad at nine o'clock for he would be there until the shepherd came back at midnight.

How easily some gave birth as the waters burst and the pointed nose and two black feet emerged from the ewe, then she licked the yellow slime from the tiny body until in minutes the lamb struggled to its feet, found the two teats and sucked gently the milk from the full udder.

We walked along the passageway between the little pens and with lantern light fed the ewes with their two, three, four-day-old lambs. The scene was magic as two hundred and fifty ewes took their turn in labour. Sometimes a ewe was in trouble when the lamb was either coming backwards or had a leg back in the womb. Then the shepherd used his skill in maternity and I was not allowed in the barn. Maybe the older folk thought I was too young to see the birth and hear the cry of pain from the mother.

At the first light of morning Shepherd Tidmarsh opened the Great Barn doors and let the in-lamb ewes into a corral-like yard bounded by thatched hurdles; down one side a long hay rack made by Jack was filled with sanfoin hay from the waggon alongside. Depending on the weather, the four-day-old lambs were driven with their mothers through the back door into another orchard where the grass grew early under the apple trees – their first light of day, to be moved again in a few days to the open field of Church Close.

The lambing finished about the beginning of April. The shepherd who had held sway in the barn spread his flock in fields near the village. Twenty ewes and thirty lambs in the First Ham, an L-shaped meadow by Carrant's Brook; twenty more in the Farm Ham adjoining; twenty in Clay Furlong (these were mainly the blue-marked sheep which had been last to give birth). The red-marked ewes would be up on Paris Hill and the Leasows with their stronger lambs.

After this was done the shepherd looked less biblical, for during the lambing he had worn a sacking pinafore-like smock, a Moses of a man in yellow corduroys. I coupled him with the prophets, but for the fact that he smoked a short clay pipe or chewed tobacco. The habit of chewing twist fascinated me, for both he and Jack the carpenter when in conversation on some deep subject would spit as they chewed, a well aimed spit which carried yards away in the orchard grass. I tried a little twist tobacco, but immediately spat it out, much to their amusement.

Tailing and castration was done only when the wind was in the right quarter and when the lambs were about three weeks old. My friend Frank (Ralph the carter's son and I) were not supposed to be present at the tailing and castrating of the lambs. Young George Earles held the lambs while the shepherd with bone-handled shut knife did the delicate operation.

The barn walls were half timbered and the squares between the beams filled with wattle and daub, the wattle being cleft oak laths, and the daub a mixture of clay, lime and cow manure, which had set like cement and been there for hundreds of years. But the barn was full of peep holes where the wattle and daub had fallen away. Frank and I watched the secret operation on the lambs from this vantage point.

It usually happened on a Saturday between nine o'clock and ten o'clock. Listening to conversations between Dad and Shepherd Tidmarsh in the courtyard when the old man fetched his wages on Friday night, I knew when the tailing and castration was to begin. The shepherd at these Friday evening meetings took on the nature of a specialist. His whole life had been spent among sheep. He lived sheep, they were a part of him, as much as his pipe and corduroys.

'How about cutting some lambs in the morning, Shepherd?' Dad would say, as a patient would ask a doctor about his child's tonsils.

Shepherd Tidmarsh would give his bronchial laugh. He was to say if the time was ripe, turning his face to the wind and looking at the starlit sky like a sailor undecided whether to put to sea. He would walk a few paces towards the stable, then come back to the court. 'Well, Master, the wind has changed, 'tis south west and that stinging wind from the east has abated. If 'tis like that in the morning I'll do the first lot, not afore nine, we don't want 'um chilled.'

Dad took two ounces of twist tobacco from his desk and handed it through the court window and said, 'Here you are, you will be wanting this.'

At nine on the Saturday morning Frank and I hid in our secret den among the leafy elder bushes near to the barn and waited. A bunch of maybe fifty ewes and their lambs had been driven from Paris Hill and penned in the barn, lambs in one pen, ewes in the other. George Earles arrived and met the shepherd by the barn doors; he was standing there with a bucket whetting his knife. 'Let's have 'um, George,' he ordered.

George caught the first lamb, a ewe lamb, and deftly its tail was cut and it ran a few yards into the orchard with little drops of blood staining the grass. The next, a ram lamb, which George held to his chest with a fore leg and a hind leg in each hand. The shepherd cut the end off what was called the purse, then, with his fingers, pulled its testicles out of their place. With his two front teeth, for he only had two, he grabbed them pincer-like one at a time until the cord broke, and put them into the bucket. All the time he chewed the twist tobacco and into each cavity where what he called the stones came from, he spat his tobacco-laced saliva as an antiseptic.

By the time he had castrated a dozen or more, his grey whiskers and drooping moustache were red with blood. Frank and I winced when we saw the ram lambs stiffen their little necks and when the operation was over walk stiffly to join their fellows. Sometimes they lay awhile on the grass stunned by the shock while others seemed to gambol away as if nothing had happened.

'The Shepherd is coming through the door. Duck,' Frank said, and we crouched down among the elders. He walked around the post operative lambs, leant on his crook and said to George, 'Oh, they'ull be alright presently,' but it was difficult to hear his words above the baaing of the ewes and the bleating of the lambs.

At about one o'clock the big doors opened and the mother ewes were reunited with the baby lambs and the little flock was left in the orchard for the day, the lambs eager for milk and sympathy from the ewes.

The shepherd tied the lambs' tails in bundles with binder twine and took his bucket with the sweetbreads to feast on the pie his wife would prepare from them.

After dinner Frank and I climbed the Pitmaston pear trees and from the holes and cracks in the huge trunks of the trees collected the sky blue eggs of the nesting starlings. I noticed the lambs didn't gang up together like race horses and circle the orchard as they had done. They never did again after the tailing and castration, but grew to be slaughtered months later, and be hung like a sacrifice in butcher's shops.

Ralph brought a muck cart to the barn and the men cleaned it of all the debris of the lambing on wet days and spread it on the grass land of Church Close by the moat pond. The dry earth floor was ready for the shearing in late May. The barn was empty for a few weeks, the hurdles stacked in a pile in one corner.

At the end of April, before the shearing, about the time of my birthday, all the ewes and lambs were brought back to the sheep fold to be 'belted'. Belting, usually known as 'dagging', was clipping the soiled wool from the breech of the ewe. The young spring grass acted as a laxative and ewes clean on the rump and breech when they went out in March would be caked with dung by late April.

Once again this weather-wise old man sniffed the wind, for the mild south westerly was just right for belting the ewes. If the wind changed halfway through the clipping of the dung hung wool, the operation was suspended. 'You see, Fred,' he'd say, 'that muck and wool does keep the bag (the udder) warm. If that gets chilled the milk dries up and we shall get garget (mastitis) among the flock.'

I've seen lots of shepherds belting or dagging ewes and have, years later, done this rather messy job myself. Never have I seen it done like Shepherd Tidmarsh. Other shepherds would put the ewe's head through a loop of rope and hold her by the left knee against a hurdle. Shepherd Tidmarsh would catch his ewe with his crook by the left leg, gently twist the crook anti-clockwise and she would come to him backwards with little fuss. He held her against a fixed hurdle, pressed his left knee into her flank then clipped the beltings from her, holding her without a loop of rope. His great corduroy-covered knee put pressure against the ewe as the soiled wool fell from his shears in a heap,

I remember saying to the shepherd, 'What will you do with the beltings?' He winked at me replying, 'Did you see my rows of runner beans and my celery last year?' Then he told me he grew everything, the potatoes and the beetroot, in the black soil of his garden on belting buried in a trench to feed his garden. Then the few gentry of the village sent their gardeners down to the Cross Barn with sacks and used the soiled wool as a fertilizer for their roses and dahlias. Some put the smelly stuff in old cider barrels,

Studying ewes under the blossom

mixed it with soot and filled the barrel with water to give liquid manure. It seemed that the beltings were just one of the shepherd's little perks. When I suggested that maybe the wool merchant from Atherstone would buy it the shepherd laughed and replied, 'Bless the fella, yer dad only gets seven pence a pound for the best wool.'

For shearing a month later Shepherd Tidmarsh spread a covering of straw on the earthen barn floor and laid a sheet down over it. His hand shears, little changed from the Middle Ages, glistened in the summer sun in the barn doorway – a far cry from mechanical clippers. They were razor sharp. His belting shears were smaller and the edge on these continually blunted by the caked muck.

At the shearing the ewe was sat down like a begging dog until the wool had been clipped from the head and the belly. Then down she went with the weight of the old man's body holding her fast. One of his legs pinioned the ewe across the neck. The shears slipped under the winter grown fleece exposing the white under the yellow of the grease in the wool. The grease was important for easy work. The shepherd's trousers were soon stiff with grease as the wool fell away like a hearth rug on the shearing floor. His shears always clipped as far as the back bone, then the ewe was turned over.

When naked she left the floor. He wound the fleece into a ball, tying it with a rope of twisted wool; it was stacked on a hurdle platform like a white Swiss roll of wool. 'Play football with a fleece, Fred boy, it'ull never come undone.' Kicking one of his fleeces proved how right his words were.

An art in shearing, an art in winding the fleece, he had gained during fifty or sixty years among sheep. It was not often that he nicked the skin of the ewe and a little blood wept from the wound. When that happened he dressed it with green oils or Stockholm tar to ward off the blue-bottle flies.

When young George Earles was helping him, his job was to stack the fleeces and mark the naked ewes. He stood there by the door dipping the marking iron into the hot tar and carefully pressed the tar-covered iron against the hip of each ewe. Like magic the letters A & B were printed so that Archer and Bailey and the shepherd could always recognize a stray sheep. The lambs soon found their mothers among the din of ewes baaing and lambs bleating and were joyfully reunited.

There was satisfaction in watching shearing done well. I wondered how long the shorn ewes would stay so white and clean, and how they felt losing all their winter clothes in fifteen minutes. Occasionally a bunch of maggots showed as the fleece was parted from the body. Then the dousing of Jeyes Fluid from a bottle called 'The Maggot Water' killed the hatched eggs of the blue-bottle-fly, and, like Robert Burns's mouse's nest turned by the plough, they lost their bed.

The great Oxford Down rams were shorn last, with George Earles holding them down for the shepherd. I'm sure he could have managed but it was usual for someone to hold the rams.

After the shearing the old thatched barn was no longer the shepherd's province. In September when the first of the apples were picked by the men they were emptied from the pot hampers into a bed of straw to lie there three feet deep until just before Christmas. On wet days the hampers were filled again from the store in the barn and the apples packed for market. The whole atmosphere of the Cross Barn changed, the smell of fruit so different from the sheep.

Before the apples were picked one bay of the barn was taken over by the casual pea pickers for their summer quarters. It was here that Scottie and Darkie stayed on beds of straw, cooking their evening meal of Fray Bentos corned beef, boiled young potatoes and green peas, over a fire. The billy cans they cooked in read 'Blue Bird toffee'. How the billy cans of tea were cooled fascinated me. Scottie would swing his billy can round and round over his head, never spilling a drop of the tea laced with condensed milk. The gentlemen of the road lived well for a few months on their shilling a pot earned in the pea field.

Like most facets of farm life, sheep begin the cycle of the year at Michaelmas. After the ewes have been flushed on good pasture, lattermath or aftermath clover (i.e. the second growth, after it had been cut for hay), they should be in tip top condition to take the ram.

We turned out the rams with the ewes on September 26th. Other folk, on land where the spring grass was late, turned out their rams on St Luke's Day (October 12th). 'On St Luke's Day let the tup have play,' is the old adage. Ewes are five months from mating to lambing.

The Kerry ewes of ours had woolly tails so Shepherd Tidmarsh sheared some wool off each side of the tail and made it narrow. A ewe in season will obligingly put her tail to one side when the ram mounts to serve her. A woolly tail can be a hindrance for the ram's penis to enter the ewe, so the shepherd sheared off a little wool.

He marked the rams with raddle on their breasts which left a red mark on the ewe's rump when she was served. Changing the red to blue after three weeks, the shepherd could tell which ewe had stood and was in lamb from the first service and if the blue went over the red, she hadn't taken the first time. We bought raddle power to make a paste with linseed oil from the chemists. Hardy writes of the raddle man, 'a frightening creature, red from head to toe from the red oxide'.

The ewes stayed all winter on the hill with the rams. They were fed hay in racks and given a little cake, locust beans, flaked maize, dried grains, a mixture Shepherd Tidmarsh made on the granary floor.

The shepherd would visit his flock at least twice a day to see if any were cast – cast being when a ewe gets on her back and is unable to get to her feet. When in lamb a ewe will soon die if cast for long.

By late January the early sprouts had been cleared, leaving the stems three feet apart in rows almost bare in the field. The shepherd with sheep wire made pens, and what were known as the 'tegs', lambs from the previous March, were put to feed on the sprout stems and the greens left by the pickers.

Every day a fresh pen was made as the tegs cleared up everything edible. The shepherd used a carving knife to split the sprout stems enabling the tegs to eat the marrow. A clean job the sheep made of the sprout field, leaving only the hard stem about six inches above the root to be dug up and burnt.

The tegs fattened on the sprout stems with hay in their racks and corn in their troughs. Every fortnight the shepherd marked a dray load to go to market, fifteen or twenty tegs, until all that were left behind were a few ne'er-do-wells which were kept until the summer and sold either fat or store.

As the folding of the tegs on the stems in the hurdle pens coincided with the early lambing in mid February, the shepherd left Bert in charge of the tegs; he did the feeding and penning now the shepherd had started lambing. But every other Monday the old shepherd walked to the sprout field, meeting Bert there. 'Catch that one, catch that one,' he said to Bert. The shepherd felt its back, its rump and marked it for market if it passed his eagle eye.

I remember a local butcher used to buy a teg every week. The shepherd marked one and when the butcher had taken it away assisted by Bert, the shepherd said, 'Did Master So and So like the teg I marked?'

Bert said, 'Oh, he reckoned the sheep was in lamb.'

The shepherd blew out his cheeks, puffed great eddies of smoke from his clay pipe and said, 'Poo, the fool, it was a wedder sheep.' A wedder being a castrated ram.

HORSES

Horses on the farm fell into three categories: the Shire type, plough and waggon animals; the half-legged, lighter type of nag used for pulling drays, light harrows, swath turners, rakes, milk floats, horse hoes, etc.; and the cob Polly for the Governess car to go to town.

By the early 'twenties the number of carthorses, Shire types, had been depleted by the war. The army commandeered some of the best of the horse flesh. We had lost both Short and Sharper, two chestnuts; what became of them in France we never knew. Ralph had often spoken to me of this pair of five-year-olds which left the farm in 1916. 'They only wanted the best to pull the transport and the guns,' he'd say with a far away look as if to say that they had got it all wrong, for shouldn't the best be on the land.

We were left with Dick and his big knee, 'And you know how occud he is,' and Captain with a ridge back like a barrel. 'What a occud squad I had in the team when the two young osses went,' Ralph told me. But Dick was saved from France by his knee. He used to hate being hitched to the big cog on the horse gearing – a big cog which turned a small cog on a shaft to the tallet or loft inside the barn where Fred Randall the cowman fed the straw into the chaff cutter. The incredible dust, the din of the shafting, the slip slap of the leather belt on the pulley and the power Dick had of turning one horse power into many more.

Dick was black with a white face but his knee was as big as a football. Daresay he'd sprained it in a rabbit hole or something I thought. Captain, despite his ridge back, was strong, an excellent filler or shaft horse for holding back the loaded waggons down Bredon Hill. But he was hard in the mouth, difficult to back with a load in the rickyard. A wily old fellow in the plough team when as filler (or the horse at the back of the team) he would run off into the ploughing instead of keeping to the furrow to pull the plough to the headland. He was bay in colour, not a handsome animal.

When the war ended, Dad and his partner Mr Bailey bought half a dozen colts and fillies at Gloucester Barton Fair. Ralph and George broke them in. First of all they put them in long gears or plough traces, with extra strong links so that when they snatched the links would hold. They hooked them to tree trunks in the meadow by the railway line and, with George holding the mullens (a blinkered bridle), and Ralph following with two plough lines for reins, they circled Didcot Ham until they lathered sweat like soap suds from their broad chests and from under the crupper. Then they were put into the four-horse scuffle or cultivator with two of the old horses.

Ralph reminiscing to me one day said, 'You know, the military took some of the best of the fodder for their horses,' I remembered the khaki-clad hay-baling company coming and cutting up a rick of clover in our rickyard which Ralph was to have to feed his horses. The rick stood thatched under the elms, sweet second cut broad red clover. A steam engine came to turn this great baling machine. An officer or N.C.O. stood by and gave the orders. Up the ladder one chap went and, pulling out the rick pegs and stripping off the thatch, began pitching the clover hay into the baling machine.

'A lazy way,' Ralph said, for he would take a hay knife and cut a rick in squares, called 'kerves', only taking off enough thatch to start what was called a cut. The knife cut the rick like a cake, straight and square.

By the early 'twenties Ralph had a good team of horses, in fact two four-horse teams. Ralph had the pick of the stable while George worked the four left behind. Ralph worked with Turpin, Flower and Violet, with old Captain as filler. Boxer, Flower's colt, came later. George had Dick, Prince, Merryman and Blackbird. Blackbird was known as a 'durgin', being on the small side, and he only had one eye. A boy with a stone blinded him one Sunday afternoon. No one ever said who did it.

How some turned their horses out for town was a picture. The brasses polished by the cottage fireplace hung from the harness. The horses' tails were plaited, strawed and ribboned. Each carter was allowed to take a couple of boltings of straw which they sold on the way to the market gardeners for them to use for covering early radish seedlings from the spring frosts; a sort of luck money for the carter.

The carthorses had their own places in the stable, they knew their place at the manger. I watched Ralph with a skip of chaff, mangolds and oat flour, cut pulped and ground in that order feed the home-coming team at night. When he opened the corn bin lid to get more corn for them then let the iron lid slam down they turned and looked at him. When he climbed the tallet ladder to the loft above to pitch clover hay into the hay rack, their heads were raised, listening to his footsteps on the tallet floor until the fodder came down from above, and, their chaff bait finished, they pulled the clover hay from the rack, before being turned out for the night.

I liked to hear them crunch the whole mangolds they had as afters in late spring when the roots were full of sugar. The sound was the magnified sound of school boys scrumping stolen apples. Better still was the sight of plough horses rolling on their backs on summer Sundays when they had their freedom; to see their shining shoes glisten in the sun and watch them rub their rumps against the horse fed elm trees or just stand in the shade as if they knew it was Sunday.

Our two half-legged nags were named Min the mare and Tom the gelding. They lived in another field from the carthorses and were stabled in the nag stable, a stable where Squire Baldwyn had kept his hunters. It had iron mangers and hay racks and the walls were tiled while by the side the harness room had a fireplace where the grooms used to live. Tom and Min pulled the two light market gardener's drays to market with loads of fruit and vegetables. They took drayloads of fat lambs to the markets of Evesham and Tewkesbury. Detachable racks could be fitted to the drays making rectangular pens for lambs and calves. At

SALLY.

haymaking these two light-legged and nimble horses pulled the swath turner to turn the hay, then the horse rake to rake it into rows – 'walleys' or 'windrows'; the mower was pulled by the carthorses.

Except in the winter months, Tom and Min pulled horse hoes among the sprouts, cabbages, peas, beans and mangolds. Their hooves being small, they walked quickly and daintily between the rows of growing crops. When Dad and Mr Bailey became partners, Min belonged to Mr Bailey while Tom belonged to Dad. He bought Tom with the first cheque he ever wrote from his account at the Capital and Counties Bank in 1907. Min was apt to fall down when climbing hilly roads so she wore a pair of leather knee pads, a cricketer on the farm.

The iron-rimmed drays of Evesham Vale of the 'twenties rattled all day long up the High Street from the land to market or the station. Some of the turnouts were smart. The brassed harness, the nag's collars and saddles always lined with a purple blue material in contrast to the black-and-white check lined collars of the cart horses. Bert, who drove Tom to market with the loads, used to have trouble up Bridge Street bank, but Eddie Davis the blacksmith was handy when the roads were icy. He screwed frost nails in Tom's shoes so that he could grip the smooth icy road.

George Earles used Min in the float to take the seventeen-gallon churns of milk to catch the 8.20 train at the station. The carthorses were the heavy goods of the day, while the nags pulled the pick-ups, and the cobs the governess car for shopping.

Polly the cob lived in Tun Flun, a corruption of Ten Furlongs, a field in front of Mr Bailey's house, with Mr Bailey's iron grey cob. Farmers drove to market in their traps and spring carts, ladies drove fast governess cars with their children. The fact was both Dad and Mr Bailey had governess cars, the Rolls Royces of the 'twenties. I liked to see the fast moving lightly sprung governess cars driven up and down the Promenade at Cheltenham competing with the electric trams. They swayed gently and the whips swung from their holsters on the off mudguards. Some folk on wet days peeped underneath coloured umbrellas. Very smart. It used to take us nearly half an hour to go the six miles to Evesham in ours; it would have been much quicker but for Sedgeberrow Bank, for Polly walked up and down that steep poplar-topped hill. Every Friday Dad and Mother drove in the polished brown rubber-tyred governess car to Evesham. Polly the mare with brown harness over her chestnut back was fast on the road, yet had a sweet temperament. She passed the smelly steam waggons loaded with corn from the dock. She rarely shied at anything. I sat in the front with Mother. Dad sat by the little door at the back with the reins, reins which were looped through two brass rings on the front of the car then through two more rings on Polly's pad saddle to her bridle. We trotted down over the station bridge to the main road. The long beige coloured trap whip pointed from its holder on the mudguard. A whip seldom used, but there just in case.

Outside the Kings Head little boys competed with each other to earn a penny to hold the farmers' cobs and nags on the cobblestones alongside the High Street. We didn't unhitch Polly from the shafts but left her in the care of one of the boys, maybe for an hour. The little boy in charge of Polly beamed a little beam of sunshine when he had the penny for looking after Polly. A

The governess cart

look of gratitude for just a little wage, an hour spent as the shadow of a groom.

I wondered why we went to Evesham with Polly the pony when the trains ran regularly from the little station. It may have been that by going to the Kings Head, the heart of the town, it saved the long trek from the station. Farmers with traps, governess cars and spring carts congregated there as they no doubt had for generations. The sight of carts with the shafts pointing upwards to the sky, while the horses baited in the Kings Head stables was commonplace, while the braying of the smallholders' donkeys, released from their carts, made me think of Biblical Palestine.

But the governess cart and Polly were overtaken by progress – the acquisition of a motor car.

It was summertime when Ponto, who slept in the granary, spent all day long polishing Polly the mare's brown trap harness. He placed the pad saddle on the court wall and I watched him clean it with saddle soap then apply the neatsfoot oil and the final polish. He Brassoed the brass squares on the blinkers of the bridle, the rings on the pad saddle; everything shone in the sunshine. The mauve blossoms of the lilac trees by the cowshed and the white lace of the elder flowers gave a scent unequalled by anything sold at Cavendish House's perfumery counter at Cheltenham.

Ponto pulled the governess car from the trap house to the daylight of the yard. He scrubbed and polished it until the grain in the wood and the spokes of the wheels looked as new. Then with Brasso he shone the hubs of the wheels and the bar where the reins had rubbed grooves in the metal as they had rested and been pulled to and fro from the driver's seat to Polly's bit.

Polly meanwhile grew fat and sleek in Ten Furlong field, no doubt wondering why she no longer took the Cheltenham road to Evesham on Friday mornings. The day after Ponto had done his cleaning and polishing, Ralph arrived with Polly on a halter and tied her up in the stable next to Min. He brushed and combed her and while he worked he made hissing noises – grooms had this little way when brushing horses. He combed her chestnut mane and tail. She looked beautiful in the shunshine as Ralph harnessed her to the governess car. Dad came out dressed in his market breeches, tweed jacket and cloth cap. I'd heard over breakfast that the turnout was to be sold. I followed Dad across the yard; he mounted from the step to the driving seat as Ralph held Polly's bridle; I patted her round rump then stroked her nose and said goodbye to what had been a part of the family ever since I could remember. I waved as Polly trotted round the corner past the pig sties, the reins loose on her back and the cane whip fawn and erect as an ash plant from the holder on the off side mudguard.

At Cheltenham Horse Repository, that grand Georgian building in Winchcombe Street, the outfit was sold, lock, stock and barrel. Dad came home by train and told Mother over tea, 'I made forty pound, Lily. I didn't like to see her go, but a farmer I know from near Tewkesbury was the buyer. She will have a good home.'

Feeling sad, I joined Ponto where he was boiling a billy can of tea by the granary steps. Ponto looked at me and said, 'You didn't like to see Polly go, Fred.' I nodded.

THE CANDLEMAS PONY

The early spring of 1926 had been marred by Dad's two weeks' stay and operation in hospital. Visits to him there in a semi-private ward with a Scot from Largs as his ward mate were accompanied by the ether smell, the heaps of clean linen, and nurses and sisters in shades of blue. The matron was a military type of lady with a heavily powdered face. When she entered the ward I had been already disciplined enough at PHGS (Prince Henry's Grammar School) to stand to attention beside Dad's bed.

Dad came out the day before Candlemas Fair. The weather was bitterly cold but a few store cattle had been entered for the sale. I walked from school at dinner time to the cattle market as usual on a Monday, meeting Dad at Restall's for a lardy cake and cocoa. He said, 'Fred, I may buy that pony for you today.' We hurried to the cattle pens and in one pen by the auctioneer's office a brown Welsh mare was nuzzling at some hay. 'A pound a leg I reckon,' Dad said with a grin, and we looked at the strings of great Shire horses, saw them put through their paces from the Railway Hotel to the Catholic Church.

Horse copers cracked whips, young cart colts reared on the

Horse copers at the fair

halter. No circus, no animal from the tropical jungle could have intrigued, impressed me like the Shire horses. Nags for market gardener's drays, nicely broken, trotted up and down the road as if in the show ring. Noisy men and boys drove colts and fillies from the horse boxes of the station to the pens. The scene was full of the noise of hooves on tarred road, of the neighing of horses, cracking of whips and the persuasive patter of the horse dealers trying to impress some farmer of the quality of the animals. I saw the dealers and the farmers rush at a prospective purchase like a boxer about to deliver a knock out blow with a clenched fist. Dad said it was to prove that the horse was not broken winded. If it was it would roar through its wind pipe.

'Get back to school now, my boy. You know what will happen if you are late.'

I half walked, half ran excitedly along Princess Road, Windsor Road into Victoria Avenue. What a royal lot we were! Then I sat bemused over maths and the master pulled me a few inches higher by the foretop of my hair. What did I care, Dad was buying me a pony.

By four o'clock Mr Righton had sold most of the horses and cattle. Tom Whittle and Bert Barnett had driven the cattle the six miles to market and they had been sold. I arrived in time to see the ponies come into the ring. The Welsh pony mare, four years old, named Kitty, was paraded round the ring under the auctioneer's rostrum. 'Start me, gentlemen, six guineas anywhere, five guineas? Thank you, four guineas. I'm selling at four guineas.' I remembered Dad saying a pound a leg and the auctioneer had been offered four pounds four shillings. They talked in guineas. Dad gave Mr Righton a nod, the hammer was posed above the well marked board and down it came. 'Mr Tom Archer, five guineas.'

'You'll take her home, Bert, won't you? There's no bridle, no saddle, do you mind?'

Bert tied the end of the halter to the other side of the webbing nose piece and made a rope rein without a bit. He threw himself across the little mare's back and was soon halfway down High Street. Dad, driving the Sunbeam, with Tom Whittle in front and me in the back, overtook Bert by the Town Hall. 'Young Bert's got no fear of the traffic, but it 'ull be dark afore he's home,' Tom commented.

In the yard as darkness fell I waited for Bert and Kitty until I heard the pair come over the Station Bridge and heard him canter up the Groaten, three half pence for two pence, three half pence for two pence. We put her in a calf pen in the barn overnight. The next day Dad found an old bridle in the harness room, too big for the mare, but he folded the straps and tied them with string until it was her size. Then he sent me down to Ernie Hine the saddler and Mr Hine altered the leathers, making a little bridle for the Welsh pony. A saddle came from somewhere, maybe from a farm sale, farm sales being Dad's recreation apart from shooting and cricket.

I'd say that Kitty was half broken in. She shied at anything in the village street, a nervous little lady, unpredictable. The first time I bit the dust was in Cottons Lane. It seemed that my grip on the reins was not hard enough to control that leathery mouth of hers. Tom took over, my big brother. He rode her to the summer house, Parsons Folly on Bredon summit, and brought her back with foaming mane and tail. I reckon they both enjoyed the trip. Tom didn't care for working horses, but he did take the nonsense out of Kitty.

PLOUGHING WITH RALPH

On leaving school at Christmas after the headmaster had forecast that I would have to farm with my feet for I had no brains, I was sent to plough with Ralph the carter, to drive four horses in line pulling a Kell single furrow plough.

At seven o'clock by the stable door in the half light of morning Ralph was putting the long gears or traces onto the team. Every horse was groomed with curry comb and brush before its collar was put on. Ralph made hissing noises as he brushed them.

'Take Captain to the water trough by the cart hovel,' Ralph said as I arrived. He had been baiting (feeding) his team since about half past five. Captain farted his way down the worn step of the stable and drank at the cold water and as he did the ball tap at the one end of the trough hissed like Ralph as the water pipe kept the trough full. Captain walked from the trough, then Flower took his place, and when all four animals had drunk I fastened their traces one behind the other, tandem fashion, ready for ploughing the Thurness Field.

The Thurness Field lay half a mile from the stable. A field shaped like a giant nose; named from 'Thor', a giant, and 'ness', a nose. 'Let's give you a leg up, byoy,' and Ralph held my hobnailed boot in one hand and I put my other foot in the trace and with a spring found myself on the broad back of Turpin, our foremost horse. Ralph walked beside the four-horse team – Turpin, Boxer his brother, and Flower the mare, the mother of them both, with old Captain of unknown parentage bringing up the rear as our filler. The team had a foremost, a lash horse, a body horse, and a filler. No one had used these terms at school and I was about to be taught by a real carter, a Victorian who spoke as Shakespeare. We were on the edge of Shakespeare country, but I had only learnt a spattering of the playwright's pen at school. Captain was honoured by the Bard's language, for in *The Merchant of Venice*, old Gobbo said, 'Thee hast got more hair on thy chin than Dobbin the fill horse has on his tail.' I marvelled at Ralph's archaic speech but at the time didn't value the words he used later to become modified by Americanisms, the OKs and the 'sez yous' aped by the boys from the cinema.

We were ploughing the stubble ready for a crop of late peas. The ploughshare only penetrated eight inches into that unyielding clay of Thurness. I walked beside the team as they plodded along like an eastern caravan. Two hundred and twenty yards, or ten chains, was the distance from the Pike Ground hedge to the ditch at the bottom end and Hammer and Length allotments.

I often wondered what Ralph was thinking as he puffed at his pipe at the plough-tails (handles). He had a sort of swaggering walk like a sailor walking the plank on a rough sea. I remember the smell of his Red Bell tobacco in early morning when the weak rays of the sun thawed the rime on the stubble and made the land so sticky. 'Don't it ever moot (stick),' he'd say, more to himself than to me, for a boy wasn't supposed to understand the trial of a ploughman.

As we turned on the headland with me walking backwards, leading Turpin by his bridle, I had to do a sort of time and motion study as Turpin turned. Boxer with tight traces helped Flower and Captain to pull the plough, then Boxer with loose traces followed the foremost and Flower took her turn to draw the

The team turns on the headland

furrow to the headland. Flower, like her sons, had to pull their 'shot' as it was called right to the boundary ditch bank and only then, with loose traces, she joined Turpin and Boxer.

'Ow, ow, ow,' Ralph called as Captain, that knowing old ridge-backed gelding, tried to leave the furrow and trespass on the ploughed land. By so doing his load was eased as the plough left the furrow and did what Ralph termed 'running off'. Loosing Turpin and running back to Captain the filler, I learnt how to lead him to the ditch bank and make a clean finish of the ploughing. By shouting 'Ow,' without avail at Old Captain, Ralph intended him to keep to the left instead of running off to the right.

Ralph then tipped his plough onto the bigger of the two wheels and it slid along the headland until I turned Turpin into the furrow and we, the four horses and Ralph and myself, were heading for the Pike Ground hedge. A peaceful job driving the plough team, the jingle of the harness and the squeak of the wheels, the snorting of the horses, and sometimes when the work went well Ralph would whistle and sing. The winter birds making for their roosts in the coppice passed over, some singly, the starlings in flocks.

'Don't them wheels holla. Fetch me the oil can from my frail basket,' Ralph would say and he squirted a jet of oil between the wheel axle and the wheel. 'Cup, come on, boy, it'll soon be shutting off time,' and with Ralph's word I clicked my tongue and our four horse power were in action.

Talking to the animals was company, but old Captain the filler was my problem. He was old and wary and didn't pull like the rest of the team. Turpin was strong and if the whip was cracked behind him he gave a sort of grunt and more than once he finished up in the hedge with me. What a lovely coat he had, like his mother Flower, the colour of chocolate. Boxer was a chestnut, while old Captain was the colour of oat straw, a light bay.

Twenty-two acres was the measurement of Thurness Field, all clay, and Ralph had often to stop the team and with a paddle, a little spade-like implement, clean the shield board or mould board. The ploughed furrows stood up behind the plough like streaks of bacon as the crows followed for the upturned worms. The birds came close behind Ralph and sometimes in front of him; they pecked out the worms as soon as the shave had exposed them.

Twenty-two acres took us more than twenty-two days to plough and by that time I knew every hedgerow tree, every headland rabbit hole, and it seemed that we should be in Thurness forever. Pictures of two horses abreast with a man with rope reins to guide them, called G.O. reins, are the usual idea of ploughing; but in the Cotswolds or Bredon Hill, two horses would be useless on the clay. No one seemed to know why the two-horse team was known as 'gee owing'; 'gee' meant for the horses to move over to the right, while 'ow' meant to the left.

After a time with Ralph, that rural Shakespeare, I picked up his sayings and his picturesque speech. 'Get up anant them osses,' translated meant, 'Get up alongside the horses.'

Ralph was a walking dictionary of archaic words. His voice was mellowed by the wind and rain and sometimes his rugged, furrowed face was reddened with cider; he never drank cider at work, always cold tea, but as a boy he had been bought at the mop or hiring fair and used to breakfast in an unlit loft of a bedroom on cider sop. The farmer didn't allow him a candle because of the risk of fire. Ralph sometimes sang behind the plough. 'The Rose of Tralee' was his special ditty. Words like 'pelf' – meaning weeds the plough share buried in the furrow – were so descriptive, yet rare apart from in the Vale. When Ralph called, 'Whoa,' it could be for various reasons. There had to be a reason for we never halted all day for what the men called 'blowings', except when the horses were sweating; then they and we had about three minutes' rest. Ralph lit his pipe and said, 'We can't do too much for a good master.'

Turpin's shoulders were known as being 'teart' or tender, so we had to be careful that his traces were even on either side so that he pulled level on his collar. 'Whoa, I'll take his traces up a link on the left side.' Ralph undid the trace from the hook on the harness and let one more link fall loose. This was to level the pull. 'Don't want to get him pinched,' Ralph observed to me and I knew that for a horse to be pinched it meant a sore shoulder under the collar, and a sore shoulder took a while to heal.

One of my jobs when we shut off, or knocked off at three o'clock was to brush the tide marks of sweat from the team's shoulders so that the hair dried clean and no dried sweat remained overnight. If we noticed a slight soreness of the shoulders, Ralph stuffed two old socks full of sheep wool and tied them a couple of inches apart under the collar. This allowed the sore to heal for the collar was kept away from the sore place when the horse tightened his traces. We kept a supply of alum in the harness house and rubbed tender shoulders to harden them. It was easy to see if a horse had been pinched by the collar – it had a sore as big as half a crown and the skin was broken. When the hair grew again, no matter if the animal was black or chestnut or bay, the new hair grew white in colour.

Young horses of three years old were known as 'green' and they sweated a lot at work on Monday mornings after a day's rest on Sunday. Some would be 'collar proud', a term used when the animal snatched and reared when the first furrow was struck until they settled for a day's work: a good description 'collar proud', for how often have boys and men felt the same on Monday mornings on a cold day at seven o'clock as the Sunday boots had been changed for hobnails and the fiery chilblains brought tears until the heels and toes of the plough boy once more accepted the trek up and down the long acres of stubble.

That winter the rain fell incessantly and the open furrows ran with water. Ralph and I put corn sacks over our shoulders to keep reasonably dry. In March the winds dried the clay, setting it like concrete. 'You got to come along a me at scuffle in the morning,' Ralph told me one Sunday as I walked the footpath past his cottage in Paris gardens.

The scuffle, or cultivator, made by Larkworthys of Worcester, had two iron wheels at the front of a square iron frame, and iron tines shod with steel tips, a heavy cumbersome implement. Ralph hitched Captain and Flower abreast into the two suppletrees or whippletrees, which were hooked into either end of a long suppletree in front of the implement. A coupling stick, a stick about one foot six inches long, with spring hooks, coupled their bridles together as joint filler horses. Turpin and Boxer were hitched in front of the pair at the rear.

Ralph guided Captain and Flower with a pair of rope G.O. lines or reins. It was my job to lead Turpin, the nearside horse, and again the four-horse team cultivated the Thurness Field. Owing to lack of frost, the clods of earth known as 'clats' were turned to be dried out by the winds of March. 'Clats as big as 'osses yuds,' Ralph observed as we sat under the hedge eating our ten o'clock bait.

It was here I realized what a clodhopper was as my feet were broken in to the rough unyielding land. It took about a week to cultivate Thurness, the roughest week of walking I remember. The winds and weak spring sunshine mellowed the fallow land until April when Dad sent Ralph and me to plough it back again. The deep furrows of the landed field were closed by the plough until the finishing of the beds, sometimes known as 'shotts', left an open top on the ridges. This exposed the clay again to the weather, thus killing the couch grass and other weeds which were greening the brown earth. A lot of man- and boy-hours in Thurness that winter and spring until both of us were sick and tired of the Thurness. The larks were nesting, the peewits cried like babies as we neared their nests, camouflaged by the soil.

Looking back, I know that the twenty-two acres would have been ploughed and cultivated by a tractor in as many hours as we spent days in the horse age of the 'twenties; but with Ralph, his philosophy, his Shakespearean talk, it was a good school in Thurness, quiet and gentle.

HENS

Mother kept about two hundred hens all on free range. Half of them, mostly pullets, were in the orchard and roosted in the black wooden henhouse with a corrugated iron roof. Adjoining the henhouse Jack Hunting, the rough carpenter, had built a scratching pen. Here on a bed of chaff the hens scratched and preened themselves on wet winter days.

I never knew why, but the hens and pullets in the orchard were light breeds, white, black, brown and Exchequer Leghorns and Anconas. When Mother fed them on a bare patch of ground under a big cider apple tree where our swing hung from two plough traces, they fled like pheasants to the corn. The Anconas fled, the Leghorns copied them with some success. In the farmyard, staid old matronly White Wyanclothes and Rhode Island Reds strutted from stable to cow shed making a nuisance of themselves when they scratched the chaff mangolds and oat flour from the cow manger. They dragged long fat worms from the muck bury, and laid their eggs in the most awkward places. One ancient cock, a type of Old English game, attacked any stranger with wings outstretched like an airplane about to take off, ruffled feathers, its heavy red-combed head well forward. A brutal beast with spurs like bayonets.

In winter Dad boiled chat potatoes (small potatoes) in the copper, mashed them with a dolly-type masher when they were cooked. These potatoes were then put in half a cider barrel to feed to the hens. The cooked potatoes were spaded out into a bucket, made into a swill with boiling water, sharps and ground oats, then were added to make the mash with a sprinkling of Karswood poultry spice – a mixture supposed to contain ground-up insects, but it had a powerful eastern spicy smell. The fowls loved it hot in their feeding troughs.

Free-range hens never laid well in the winter but, with Karswood spice and mash and the luxury of the scratching pens, the light breeds in the orchard laid pretty well. They had nest boxes lined with straw so their eggs were clean, while the old dames of the muck bury which roosted on the beams in the barn on the hay loader laid their eggs under mangers. Their eggs had to be washed for sale. For some years our eggs went to Fullers of Birmingham on the milk train with the milk. They were packed in large egg boxes like cabin trunks. Each box must have held many dozens of eggs. Prices ranged from nine pence [3½p in today's money] a dozen in the spring when eggs were plentiful to one and three pence [6p] a dozen in winter.

Gone broody

Sometimes Mrs Bowles arrived, driven by a tall thin man in a Ford lorry with a canvas tilt, a covered waggon affair. Mrs Bowles was in the market for eggs and would come every week to collect and pay cash. She usually came about dinner time. The tall, thin, pale-faced lorry driver loaded the eggs while Mrs Bowles paid. She had a large black leather handbag and a purse full of notes and silver. Collecting eggs around the farms and selling them in Birmingham seemed to earn her a decent living; she was always well dressed. What the relationship was between her and the driver no one knew – it was her business. She referred to him as Alf. Egg collecting from Mother's hens was fraught with danger when the angry broody hens sat tight under the mangers. The broodies were hard to dislodge. They threatened me and took chunks of flesh from my hands when I evicted them. Armed with a rick peg I poked at them, then, if they refused to budge, Frank and I would carry a squawking bird to the horse trough and sit it on the water, hoping to cure its broodiness so it became a useful laying bird again. The usual, more humane practice was to shut them in a pen with a slatted floor so that sitting was uncomfortable.

But the sight of a broody hen with her chicks scratching for worms on the muck bury (manure heap) was more natural than the chicken brooder. Dad bought one which held about one hundred day-old chicks which we fetched from Mr Pearson of Gretton Fields. All balls of yellow fluff, packed in boxes to be reared by a paraffin lamp with a gauze around it. Every evening after the chicks had been fed the lamp was trimmed and filled with paraffin and the wick turned up just high enough to be the right temperature for the chicks. When the wind blew the lamp was liable to go out and we found the birds looking cold and miserable around a doubted lamp. Then one night the lamp was burning too high and the brooder filled with smoke. I remember seeing one hundred chicks that should have been pale yellow, as black as sweeps from the smoke. I never liked the brooder after that, it seemed so unnatural compared with the broody hen and maybe twelve chicks under her wings safe from the weather, safe from the rats.

Our multitude of cats never killed any chickens, but a neighbour's cat from the cottage next to the pub was a menace. One hundred Light Sussex pullets arrived one day from Mr

Pearson's poultry farm; eight weeks old they were and were put in a wire pen in the rickyard. Every day one was missing.

It was a June night when Dad waited with his twelve bore gun hiding with me by the milk cooling hut. A great tabby crossed the yard carrying a pullet, and bang, her whole nine lives ended on the farm roadway. We buried her in the muck bury, the end of anything which offended in the feline line. The remainder of the pullets grew into laying hens and joined the Rhode Island Red cockerels to lay eggs and eventually to breed what were known as sex linked poultry, for when the chicks were hatched the pullets were brown and the cockerel chicks were white.

CROPS

'For everything there is a season, a time to sow, a time to reap,' so it says in *Ecclesiastes*.

There is a lore of the market gardener and farmer, a time to plant everything. Early peas we planted at Candlemas (February 2nd), if it was drying weather; mangolds on Lady Day, March 25th; runner beans, Stow Fair, May 12th, or when the elm leaf is as big as a farthing. It was time to plant runner beans in the garden when the elm leaf is as big as a penny. Asparagus was cut from late April or early May until Pershore Fair, June 26th. It was grown in ridges three feet apart and when cut three inches under the ground, the bud was white at the bottom. Good Friday was the day to plant early potatoes, no matter whether Easter was early or late. Gooseberries picked green for Whit Sunday dinner. The Evesham market gardeners used to walk up Clarks Hill above the Avon at twelve o'clock on March 21st and see which quarter the wind came from for it was said whatever the wind was then it stayed there for forty days.

Strawberry picking was a four o'clock in the morning job for the farm workers and their wives. Monday morning's market at Cheltenham started at six thirty so by six o'clock Dad had loaded the Sunbeam car minus its back seat with twenty-four trays of one pound punnets.

No one worked on Sundays so Monday's sale was a race between the growers to get the most picked for the early Monday auction. We grew Bedfords, Sovereigns and Paxtons and these choice berries would make one shilling [5p] a pound on Monday morning, bought often by Stephen Sharpe who kept a select fruiterer's shop in the Promenade. Some were taken by Bert on the horse dray to the eleven o'clock sale in Evesham, but there the price would be more like sixpence [2½p] a pound. I used to go to Cheltenham with Dad those early Monday mornings before school, then come home to breakfast.

GILLY FLOWERS, SPRING ONIONS AND ASPARAGUS

As a boy I questioned why wallflowers were called gillies, for didn't the old rhyme go: 'Hot July brings cooling showers, apricots and gilly flowers.' Our gillies were dark red wallflowers picked in March and April. Five acres of sweet, perfumed blood red blooms gave spring a special meaning in the village, gillies having been planted between the yard wide rows of autumn sown Seville beans in the previous May. What a scene on a June morning when the giant Seville beans were picked by the travellers of the road, the diddeycoys (itinerant gypsies), and the village women.

The bean harvest came before the early peas. The haulm, known as 'bean brish', was left in the rows stripped of the pods, between the struggling gilly plants. There was a reason for planting the seed between the beans, for the beans protected the seedling gillies from the turnip fly.

Leading Flower the mare in a dray, I would steer her between the rows of young gilly plants while a couple of men raked and forked the haulm into the dray which when loaded was taken to the headland to be burnt. The field was often a mass of thistle, chickweed, groundsel and all the common weeds of summer. How could these young and tender plants survive to give a picturesque pattern on the bare countryside of March? But this practice had withstood the test of time. Many farmers who took up market gardening in the depression years of the early 'thirties copied the small gardeners of the Vale.

Under the hot July sun when the rhyme recorded apricots and

gilly flowers, our spring flowering gilly plants had to be cleaned of the weeds with a skim plough, a type of horse hoe developed by Burlinghams of Evesham. 'You'd better start skimming the gillies in the morning, Ralph,' Dad would say to the carter at the stable door. 'Alright, Master, but I'll want young Fred to lead the 'oss, 'cos you know I won't be able to manage with a pair of reins.'

Ralph's eyebrows were raised even higher than usual as he anticipated a few days of hard work cutting the weeds with the two knife-like shares of the skim plough. 'He will be along at seven o'clock, Ralph, and I'll come and see how it goes.' Ralph nodded, not relishing at all the job in prospect. Then he sent me to Tom Higgins the blacksmith on my bike to get the shares sharpened. Tying the two shares on the cross bar of my bike, I set off to the blacksmith's shop.

'They be blunt, Fred byoy, I could ride bare arsed to London on 'um without being cut. They 'udn't cut butter avout they were red hotted.' The blacksmith's man Bill Slatter put the shares in the fire one at a time and I pumped away at the bellows, holding the cow horn handle until the fire glowed. Bill with his tongs moved the iron around in the fire until the metal was white hot. On the anvil he thumped away with his hammer at the inch wide edge of the share and it became wafer thin at the extreme edge. Hammer in right hand and tongs in left, he rained blows on the iron, working as he did from left to right along the edge of the share.

Meanwhile the other share lay among the coal on the fire which had daumered until it appeared almost dead. Now the bellows were silent. Bill picked up the share with his tongs and plunged it deeply into the stone trough of water then took it out quickly and held it to his face. It steamed and the white hot metal turned to a bluish tint. He then plunged it once more into the water to get the right temper on the metal and dropped it on the stone floor of the shop.

When the other share had had the same treatment, Bill carried the two sharpened knife-like parts of the skim plough to his vice and gently rasped the edges with a file until neither Ralph nor anyone else could have ridden on them bare arsed to London.

Next morning Ralph bolted the shares into the feet of the skim plough and we took Boxer to the gilly field. Ralph set the two wheels rather deep so that the shares could cut the thickest weeds away from the hard sun-baked ground. 'Go ahead,' Ralph ordered, his pipe puffing eddies of smoke above the headland. I steered Boxer up between the first two rows of gillies, rows difficult to discern amid the wilderness of weeds. The skim slid under what Ralph called the pelf until the whole rectangular frame was full of weeds. It was reeving the weeds into a heap. I looked back and saw a clean aisle between the first two rows of plants.

'Whoa,' Ralph called, but Boxer didn't need telling twice. He halted while Ralph raised the tails or handles of the skim above his head, leaving a heap of cut weeds underneath. 'Go ahead,' Ralph called. So with the tails still above his head for a yard, a heap of weeds lay like an unlit bonfire behind. Ralph dropped the skim again and we went another ten yards or so and the same thing happened again, skimming weeds and leaving the heaps behind until we reached the far headland.

Dad arrived just before our ten o'clock bait, always encouraging Ralph and complimenting him on making the best of a difficult and hard job. Beads of sweat ran down Ralph's weatherbeaten face and down his bared arms. 'My Goy, Master, what a devilish job, and don't it ever give my arms summat. I shall have to have blowings today on the headland (a short rest) or else you'll have me on the Box (on the sick list).'

Ralph's arms were slim, his whole body on the spare side, but I saw in him a man of mettle not easily beaten. As we rested on the headland he would tell me of the ulcer he suffered from and how he took Macleans Powders for it. Then the persistent eczema on his arms. He spoke of his doctor as being no better than some 'apple 'ooman'. Sometimes I left Boxer and helped him to free the skim of weeds, all the time admiring him, his will power, his dedication to work until the field was finished, and once more the horse and dray hauled the weeds to the headland while the men followed and hoed the rows of gillies.

By then the gilly plants, despite their rough birth, were growing, but there were gaps in the rows. On wet days the men pulled handfuls where the crop was thick and used them for what was known as 'mending', gapping up the bare places and planting the young plants with setting pins.

Depending on the winter, the first blooms were fit for marketing in March. I see the women cutting the flowers and tying them in bunches with raffia, see them as if it were yesterday.

They carried the bunches to the headland in their hurden aprons where one of the men packed them in hampers for market.

As dray loads were sent by rail to Nottingham, I wondered where they went, what the flowers were used for. Some said they made perfume while others said they were used for dye. That seemed to me more reasonable, for any yellow petals among the flowers were frowned upon; the gillies had to be dark red. In the season the women worked hard, for they were only paid one penny [½p] for picking and tying a dozen bunches. One Saturday when there was no work for the horses I tried my hand at gilly picking and worked all day picking twelve dozen bunches for one shilling [5p].

The season was over in late April, and then Ralph took two horses abreast on the big skim plough cutting the spent plants to be harrowed up in heaps and burnt. Nothing was ploughed in if it

An apron of gilly flowers

87

could be burnt. The smell of fires, couch grass fires, from gardens, farms and allotments was smelt all through the year. There was something pleasant about a garden fire at dusk when the smoke eddied around the cottages as the cottagers often burnt the earthen paths and made a path from the red ashes.

One year an acre of gillies was let run to seed for a local seed merchant. The sheaves of gilly seed hung to dry in the granary on the beams until a wet day when it was threshed on the floor with rick pegs. A noisy, dusty job made even noisier by Frank and me. We knelt alongside Uncle George, Dad's older brother, who lived in the village, and beat out the seed from the pots chanting, 'There ain't no sense sitting on a fence, all by yourself in the moonlight.' Uncle said we charmed him to death almost, but to beat out to a popular song made the hours pass quickly.

The seed and chaff was then winnowed in a fashion as old as time. Between the stable and the granary a narrow passageway was always draughty. The wind blew like the blacksmith's bellows. I watched one of the men pour the mixed chaff and seed from a peck measure. He poured it onto a sheet from high above his head so that the seed fell on the sheet while the chaff blew away. Surprising how effective this way of winnowing was. When the seed was poured down a second time it lay like little golden coloured tiny beads on the sheet, clean and ready for the seed drill.

The granary, known as the ball room, for dances had been held there long before village halls were common, was a haunt for us boys catching sparrows or shooting them with our air guns. Sometimes we lay quiet and shot a rat or a mouse. There was always life in the granary. From the nag stable below on winter days when snow covered the yard we set our primitive trap for birds, mostly sparrows. A sieve or riddle at one side with a short stick was placed over some chaff and tail (small) wheat. A length of binder twine fastened to the stick led to the nag stable door where we waited until the birds were under the riddle. A sharp snatch on the string brought the riddle down on top of the unsuspecting birds. Just a Saturday afternoon bit of sport for Frank and me when sparrows were hungry and too numerous. If we caught a robin that was released. Robins didn't raid the corn ricks or the growing corn on the headlands. Starlings we killed for they ate the strawberries.

Spring onions spelt backache from weeding, hoeing and even pulling, when backs were bent double. The men used short-sticked hoes to fiddle the groundsel, the chickweed between the rows. No man of worth ever hoed onions with a long sticked hoe. It could be done, but tradition declared that backs must be bent double to hoe onions properly. The men pulled the onions in the spring and took them in hampers to what was known as the 'gras house', 'gras' being the Evesham name for asparagus. Sitting in a circle on wicker pot hampers the women tied with onion string the salad onions in little bunches for a halfpenny [¼p] a dozen bunches . . . Dad's partner, Mr Bailey, bunched them, a dozen bunches in a pack, tied with a withy twig. My job was to wash the dozens in a long tank of water until the white slender bulbs and the string-like roots were as white as snow, then to pack the dozens in hampers for market. Mrs Heath was an expert onion tyer. Her fingers moved like knitting needles as she tied the bunches, which fell from her apron onto the brick floor of the gras house.

Asparagus has always been considered a luxury vegetable but two thousand acres grew on the clay lands around the Vale when I was a boy, and half a crown [12½] for a bundle of one hundred buds was a good price. But a hundred buds of asparagus was in fact one hundred and twenty buds, known as a long hundred, like the bakers' dozen of thirteen. It was all hand work growing asparagus. It was the winter of 1928 when I foolishly asked Mr Bailey if Frank and I could try our hands at alleying out the gras. The rows were three feet apart but the clay land was dug in between as spit by spit the forkfuls of clay were placed to form a ridge above the dormant roots of gras. 'Here you are, my boys, two new two prong digger forks from Averal's of Evesham.' Frank and I held the new tools and looked at each other as much as to say, the mens' forks are worn, ours are new.

We joined the gang in Beckfords Way where they worked, apparently with ease, moving backwards as they left the sods of clay forming a neat ridge. Starting on the headland in line with the men we dug our tools deep into the putty-like clay and placed the spits of soil on the top of the ridge where the stubble from the last year's bower or fern marked the rows. Soon our jackets were on the hedge as the sweat began to make the sleeves cling to our unseasoned arms. Then our waistcoats were abandoned as we struggled to keep up with the men. Old Uncle George laughed and said, 'You hobbledehoys have got a lot to learn.'

After dinner I took our forks to the blacksmith's and asked him to crank them like the other men's forks to ease the work. We struggled on until nearly five o'clock, then I watched Uncle George, how he dug his fork into the clay almost at forty-five degrees while we were doing a ninety degree job. 'Watch Uncle George, Frank,' I whispered as we were yards behind the gang. Learning the hard way is often the right way, for by following Uncle George's maxim and not digging so deep, the next day the art of alleying out gras was mastered.

Cutting buds of gras

Seven acres of gras standing with buds like rows of soldiers on a hot Monday morning in May is not a formidable task for twelve or fourteen men and boys. We never cut the buds on Sunday so Monday was the big cut. With sharp knives, the prongs shaped like the fingers of the hand, a long prong at one end of the knife and the little finger-like prong at the other, I learnt how to cut asparagus, grasping the bud with the left hand between finger and thumb then sliding the knife at forty-five degrees under the bed. The left finger told us when to push the knife under the bud just by the feel or tickle between finger and thumb. It was important to cut about three inches below the surface so that the end of each stalk was white.

Tying the gras was done in the gras house by the women. They placed the buds in a half-open box; with the best buds on top of the box, they tied thirty buds with raffia. The hundreds of asparagus were bundled by one of the men who put the bunches on a table and secured four bunches under a piece of webbing which formed a loop over the table from two holes in the table. The other end of the loop of webbing was about four inches from the floor. A foot on the loop kept the bunches in place so that the bundler could tie the hundred with an osier or withy twig.

By keeping the best buds of the gras on the outside, the finished hundred looked so much better in the market. It seemed dishonest to me as a boy, but everyone in the Vale bundled in that way, the shopkeepers knew that.

On June 26th, when the cuckoo was supposed to ride a horse away from Pershore Horse Fair, cutting ceased. The buds still

November: the starling's feast

91

showing grew into a bower or fern. What a picture that was in autumn when the starlings feasted on the red berries of the bower and went late to their roost in Hinton Roughs. The bower was cut with bagging hooks, smooth edged sickles, in October. Some gardeners burnt it, but we were a mixture of farmers and gardeners so our bower was hauled to the mangold field to shield the mangold bury (heap) from frost. In the winter when digging the ridges an overnight gultch of rain didn't stop the work for the men sowed lime over the clay to prevent it sticking to the boots and the forks. From Christmas until Christmas there was work among the gras.

HAY MAKING

Early in June Ralph cut the sainfoin hay by the Great Hill barn on the plateau of Bredon Hill. Sainfoin, which means 'holy hay', was first grown on the Cotswolds about two hundred years ago, the seed imported from France: we grew it mostly in permanent leys. Its red clover-like flower was so pretty, like a miniature lupin and the hay made good fodder for the shepherd's ewes.

Sainfoin in bloom

Elder-flowered bridles ward off the flies

Ralph had a Bamford mowing machine pulled by two horses. Turpin and Boxer were his favourites.

He rose about four in the morning and started mowing at five when the dew was heavy on the hay field; he worked there alone with just the peewits and larks as company. The swaths fell before the agitating mower knife which rattled between the fingers of the machine. As the sainfoin field was octagonal in shape the first swath under the dry stone walls followed that pattern. Round the field Ralph rode on the iron seat, padded with a little sack of hay, every circle becoming smaller until the last acre of red flowers looked like a cottage garden, with the wilted swaths drying and changing colour hourly in the sun. When the sun made the machine pull harder for the sweating horses, Ralph would hook them off, eat his midday dinner and rest them until evening.

In the afternoon George and Tom would climb the hill with a load of straw on a waggon to make a staddle for the sainfoin rick near the barn. The staddle, a foundation of straw, was to keep the valuable fodder off the damp ground.

When the sainfoin had been mown Ralph mowed the Brookside meadows and it was here the horses were plagued with horse flies known as old maids. Ralph laced elderflowers in the horses' mullens or bridles to keep the flies from their eyes: a picture so rural, so ancient, of horses coming towards us camouflaged in elder with Ralph on the mower seat driving his two-horse team with G.O. lines or rope reins.

While Ralph was mowing the Dewrest field by Carrants Brook, his son young Frank circled the field on the hill with a swath turner, a Martins machine which turned the swaths over, letting the sun and wind turn a green leaved, red flowered crop to pale green, sweet smelling hay. With two Lion ten-foot wide horse rakes, Frank and I raked the swaths into walleys or windrows where it would lie to dry for up to a week in straight lines wide enough apart for the broad-wheeled waggon to travel between the rows when the hay was fit to carry.

The hay pitchers came, usually George and Fred, and Tom the cowman's son. Hay pitching, with long shafted three-pronged pitchforks called shuppicks, a corruption of the word sheafpike, was a skilled craft. Little Uncle George stood on the waggon with a shorter fork and loaded it. I led the horse between the rows and called out, 'Hold tight,' to Uncle every time we moved on.

He told the pitchers where he wanted every forkful to be placed and after the bed of the waggon was full he put first of all corners on the front on top of the raves or sideboards. 'Corners on the front,' he called. Fred put one corner on while George put a pitchful to make a corner on his side. 'Now some in between um,' Uncle called. That bound the corners on.

'Corners on the back,' and the same age old process was repeated.

'Pitchful behind the front corners.' The pitchers obliged.

'Over,' Uncle ordered like a cricket umpire. This meant pitch the hay in the middle of the load under Uncle George's feet. He trampled the hay down. The pitchers told him if one side overlapped the waggon and was a bit heavy.

'A bit heavy on my side, Uncle,' Fred would say and push the side of the load in with his fork.

Sometimes four pitchers were pitching the hay then Jack Hunting the rough carpenter joined Uncle George on the load. He was normally a gentle soul but when he had been on the cider he became what Dad called 'conterary', so that if the horses snatched when they moved on he called to me, 'Let 'um go. Steady boy, and call out, "Hold tight", or you will throw us arse over head off the waggon.'

Mr Bailey sometimes was one of the pitchers and was always in a hurry, looking at the weather for signs of rain or thunder storms. 'Looks black over Bill's Mother's, Master Bailey.' This warning from George speeded the work more. Bill's Mother's, I gathered, was on the Cotswold Edge at Winchcombe.

Meanwhile Jack Barnett would be unloading the waggons at the rick to Dad, Walt and Tom Whittle, who built the rick as if it was a house to stay for ever, rectangular, upright. When hay was stacked in the rickyard, a staddle or foundation was made of faggots of wood or straw, on the stone floor of the rickyard. If the hay was stacked in the field, a sheltered dry spot was chosen under a hedge. In that case a staddle of straw was the only foundation, and when the rick had been used up the following spring, the straw left would be burnt and the site of the rick tidied up, a temporary site compared with the permanent site in the rickyard.

Ricks were often built of twenty tons of hay. The stepping out of the site for the rick in the field was done by Tom the cowman.

Corners on the front

He and Dad looked at the crop of hay and assessed how many waggon loads there were. Four pegs or stakes were driven into the ground, representing the corners of the rectangular rick, ten or twelve yards by five or six yards. The staddle of straw was laid. Boltings (big sheaves of straw) trussed with two bands of binder twine were laid along the edges of the staddle, more straw, loose straw, even mouldy straw, pitched from a waggon into the middle of the staddle.

The first load of hay pitched down by a man from the waggon drawn alongside the rick was fed to the rick builder whose concern it was to build the edges straight from stake to stake. On a fair sized rick three men would work: the rick builder, another man who took the hay from the unloader and one who scattered the hay in the middle of the rick keeping the middle full and feeding the builder with hay. When the hay rick reached a height when the man unloading the waggon had difficulty in pitching the forkfuls of hay onto the ever growing rick, the elevator pole was used, or the monkey pole with grabs. The pole, like a giant fishing rod, was laid on the floor with the butt end in the middle of the side of the rick. It had four long ropes fixed to the top of the pole and an arm called a jib which had two pulley wheels, one at the pole end, one at the other end of the jib. A rope from a pulley at the base of the pole was threaded through the two pulleys on the end of the rope where the grab forks hung. The other end of the rope lay alongside the rick with a chain on its end for a horse to pull forward when the grabs were pushed into the hay on the waggon and the jib would swing and a trip cord, operated by Jack, opened the grabs and the hay fell in a huge forkful at the feet of the builders.

First of all the pole was raised upright, but slightly leaning towards the rick. This was a job for about six men. The pole was lifted onto half a load of hay, then the shaft horse was backed until the pole was rearing upright. One man held each one of the four guy ropes and pulled and held according to what Dad said as he pushed and pulled at the bottom of the pole. 'Pull, George, not too much. Pull, Fred. Steady.' The pole swayed until in upright position the four guy ropes were fastened to four long iron pegs and two pegs were driven into the ground at the butt of the pole.

My job now was to lead Captain as he elevated the forkfuls of hay. I walked backwards with an eye on the jib until the forkfuls of hay swung on the rope over the rick and were tipped. The jib swung them over the waggon, the empty forks above Jack's head. 'Hold back,' Jack called, and I backed that hard mouthed gelding until the forks rested at Jack's feet on the load. What a job, backing Captain, see-sawing at his bit as he unwillingly backed along that rickside track. As the rick grew the jib was highered on

The monkey pole (automation in the 'twenties)

a rope which held it on the pole until the last load was built into a ridge and the cottage-like rick was finished. A line of boltings (trusses) of straw put along the ridge of the rick finished the building, which was thatched a month later to protect the fodder from the rain.

After the pitchers had loaded the last load, Frank and I raked the field again to gather up the last wisps of hay. Together we rode over two hundred acres of hay fields one year on the hard iron seats of the horse rakes. These rakes had a lever which we pulled every time we tipped the hay into walleys. Raking over the second time was easy because the windrows were far apart, but every mouthful of hay was saved.

When the hay was weathered in a wet summer Tom and Ralph would say, 'Oy, the cattle would sooner eat this stuff in the winter than their fore feet or a snowball.' How right they were, but, as the saying goes, 'Good hay has no fellow.'

CORN

Because of the cheapness of Canadian wheat, which could be bought delivered at eight shillings [40p] a hundredweight, the acreage of wheat we grew diminished while the acreage of oats increased: oats to feed the sheep, the cattle and the horses.

Winter wheat, usually the Square Heads Master variety, was planted after a clover ley in early October; the wheat would be followed by a root crop. A Knapp nine row drill pulled by two horses planted the grain. The seeding was one and a half hundredweight per acre. The Knapp drill had a wooden seed box above the nine legs from which the seed trickled into the feet or coulters which drilled the seed about two to three inches under-ground. The drill had shafts for a shaft horse. In front of the shaft horse a boy (often me) led a trace horse. Ralph the carter walked behind the drill holding a pair of reins which led to the shaft horse or filler. He had to watch the grain run from the box as the cogs fed it down the spouts or legs. If one spout got clogged with straw or something Ralph called, 'Whoa,' and we cleared the spout to avoid a telltale gap, a bare piece of land where a row of corn should have come up.

We could drill nine acres a day, an acre for every row the drill planted. A man would follow us and harrow (and cover) the seed bed. He would drive two horses which pulled three harrows. These horses would work abreast with the man walking behind the harrows holding the reins.

The Knapp nine furrow drill was futuristic in the 'twenties. Lots of farmers still planted their corn with a five row drill pulled by two horses abreast. This drill had rigid wooden legs as opposed to the sprung legs of the Knapp. It also had tails or handles like a plough which the carter held, bearing on heavily where the ground was hard, and lightly where there was a deep mould or tilth.

In late March when the sprout field had been cleared of the stems, Ralph skim ploughed the land with a heavy two horse skim which preserved the sugary frost mould of three inches on top of the clay without bringing the clay in lumps to the surface. The resultant tilth was ideal for spring wheat planting or spring oats.

There seemed to be only one variety of spring wheat, French Marvel. This we grew mainly for fowl corn for our poultry and

Riding the foremost horse

Mr Bailey's at the Old Manor Farm. Victory White oats was the sort which suited our land, the grain and straw making good feed for the animals. When the wheat price was so low I doubt if we would have grown any but for the fact we needed the straw to thatch the hay ricks and for bedding for the cattle.

When the wheat was ready to harvest, a man cut a road around the cornfield so that the three horses on the reaper or binder could cut the first swath; then Ralph put Turpin and Flower in a pair on each side of the pole of the Massey Harris machine and Boxer was hitched onto the end of the pole in front of the other two. I rode Boxer and Ralph drove the two behind from his seat on the binder. It was like a mowing machine with an endless belt of canvases carrying the cut corn from a bed behind the knife where the rotating sails pushed it in straight lines on the binder bed. The canvases carried the corn with the ears at the back under a semi-rotary fork which had a string of binder twine laying underneath and by some weight mechanism the tier tied a knot in a sheaf and the fork pitched it onto the stubble. Here the sheaves lay in lines to be stooked in sixes by the men, putting them in rows like the aisle of a church. A tidy job and how I liked riding Boxer all day with Ralph on the binder seat.

When I was a boy most of the sheaves of wheat or oats were stacked in the Dutch barn, but I remember ricks on staddle stones in Stanley Farm rickyard. These mushroom looking stones, now garden ornaments, were the foundations of corn ricks. The stones formed the outline of a rectangle or sometimes a circle. One capped stone at each corner, then at intervals they stood like a mushroom graveyard when the rickyard was bare in summer. Long planks of wood made a framework which criss-crossed the staddle or foundation. Then faggots of wood formed the first layer of the building before the whole area was covered with straw.

To build a rick in the first instance a stook of sheaves was made in the middle with the ears of corn uppermost. More sheaves were built against the stook until the first layer of sheaves had been placed with the ears of corn uppermost. This was to protect the first layer from any rising damp. Then the builder circled the rick on his knees, keeping the butt end of the sheaves always to the outside and binding one row on top of another, laying them horizontally. He finished each course in the middle of the rick and then the ears of corn dipped towards the ground with the butt ends uppermost.

When it was decided to roof the rick, he began to draw in every course of sheaves a little from the outside and every course became narrower until the ridge was made with a couple of rows of sheaves, then covered with some boltings of straw until it was thatched.

Tom, our late cowman, told me that as a ploughboy after work in the field, his job after harvest was to crawl underneath the elevated staddles with a pair of sheep shears and clip any hanging pieces of straw which reached from the rick above to the ground so that the mice had no ladder to climb and get into the rick.

Ricks on staddle stones were built for two reasons. To keep out the rats and mice who would be unable to climb the stones when they reached the mushroom umbrella stone. And to prevent the

Home and dry on staddle stones

corn from getting damp or mouldy through rising damp from the rickyard floor. Threshing took place in winter, when there was time to do it, but when a farmer needed the money to pay the Michaelmas rent a rick would be threshed in September.

THRESHING THE CORN

It took at least seven men and boys to work a threshing machine. A dusty job in winter when the days seem longer than summer. Joe North brought the machine with a steam engine from Winchcombe – a caravan of an engine, threshing machine and straw tier.

He drew alongside the Dutch barn, jacked the threshing box as he called it, until the spirit level on its side showed the bubble dead centre. He came on a bike next day and got up steam from the heap of steam coal Ralph had hauled from the station. A hose pipe sucked the water from a half cider barrel alongside.

At seven o'clock in the half light of day he blew the whistle. The engine with its long belt started turning the threshing machine. The smell of steam, the smoke and the rotating governors on his engine as the machine hummed, more, more, more, and the brass on the engine shone in the light of the fire box as he shovelled coal into the glowing fire. The engine rocked slightly, the long driving belt flapped as the big flywheel turned a small pulley and the engine multiplied the revolutions on the threshing drum.

Joe's partner fed the sheaves, after Bert had cut the strings, into the gaping hole of the drum. Soon corn flowed into the sacks at the engine end of the machine and the shakers on the end of the threshers shook the threshed straw into the straw tier. The straw tier made boltings tied with two strings then kicked them out to a man who pitched them to another man building the straw rick. Uncle George wheeled the full sacks of grain into the nearby granary and weighed them on a dead weight weighing machine, two hundredweight and a quarter in each sack.

Jack and Fred pitched the sheaves to Bert the bond cutter who cut the strings and then fed them into the machine. Boys, including me, carried the chaff which fell under the machine into the barn. My first job was carrying water with a yoke and two buckets to keep the water butt full for the engine. Then I helped Shepherd Tidmarsh to build the straw rick.

The whole day was mechanical, no let up as the machine called more, more, more, and when an uncut sheaf fell into the drum the steam engine answered with a chuff, chuff, chuff, with steam and smoke rising into the nearby walnut trees.

When the corn from the bay of the barn was finished at dusk then the rats began to run: rats which had sheltered for the winter, warm and fed to be killed by little boys with sticks and terrier dogs.

Threshing with a steam engine was picturesque to an onlooker, but reminded me of the treadmill, endless, no time to stand and stare; sweat, dust and chaff under our shirt collars.

The wheat in the two and a quarter hundredweight sacks was bought by West Midland Farmers, an early co-operative. The 'tail' or small wheat was kept to feed the hens along with some of the spring sown French Marvel wheat. Ralph loaded the sacks of wheat onto a waggon and put them in trucks at the station for the buyers to unload at Gloucester.

The oats were kept in the granary on a wooden floor to be shovelled into sacks when they were needed for animal feed and taken to be ground into flour at Sedgeberrow water mill.

When corn growing diminished, many farmers in the Vale of Evesham started market gardening, growing sprouts and peas mainly. We always had grown a fair acreage of these crops.

SPROUTS

Brussels sprouts, which were a main crop in the Vale in the 'twenties, had been, up until the turn of the century, only grown in gentlemen's gardens and by small growers. Dad and his partner grew about forty acres when I was a boy. They were the first growers to grow sprouts on the limestone hills of Bredon in 1911, a dry year when under the stones the land was damp and cool.

Archer and Bailey had their own strain of sprouts and sold their seed all over the country at one pound per pound. It was my job to weigh and package sprout seed and post it. Bredon Hill where the seed was grown was well away from other crops of the cabbage family where the bees could cross-pollinate the seeding sprouts. Dad and Mr Bailey chose an acre of sprouts at the far end of a fifteen-acre field. The sprouts had been cleared everywhere by March, all but this selected acre. Here the sprouts on top of the stems were left unpicked and they burst into greens. These greens would blossom yellow and then produce the seed pods. In an acre of sprouts there would be some stems that were known as wild, not true to type. These stems were marked with nut sticks by Dad and his partner. The men pulled them up before they flowered. A simple form of selection where only the best stems were left to seed.

The seed was gathered in the autumn and tied in sheaves, taken to the granary and hung up to dry. A two hundredweight sack of seed stood underneath the inglenook at our house and here on winter nights I weighed the seed.

Sprout picking can be a cold job in winter, but our men picked piece work and doubled their day's wages, finishing work at four o'clock.

The seed planted in Mr Bailey's garden in February came up after some weeks and then the chaffinches would be busy feeding on the young plants. Another of my jobs as a boy was shooting finches with a number three garden gun and keeping the flocks of them off the seedlings. By May the plants would be ready to transplant. They were planted by setting pins (or dibbers) three feet apart each way, planted on the square so that they could be horse hoed each way. We marked the land out, George and I, with an adapted steerage horse hoe frame with a long tool bar with four legs a yard apart. When the field had been marked out one way, we marked it at right angles so that where the two marks crossed the men with their setting pins transplanted a plant. This way there were four thousand eight hundred and forty plants per acre.

A good man could plant with his setting pin one acre per day. The land had previously been manured with either fish manure, meal and bone or hoof and horn. A top dressing of sulphate of ammonia was given to each individual plant about a month after planting, a teaspoonful to each plant.

All the summer the horse hoe kept the land clean apart from a little square around each plant which the shears or feet of the horse hoe was unable to cut. This was hoed by men using hand hoes. If early sprouts were being grown the plants were topped in late August so that the sprouts at the bottom of the stem were soon fit to pick. Topping sprouts meant pinching a small piece of green from the middle or crown of the plant which stopped the plant growing any higher. The first pick in September came in the pleasant weather of autumn. To keep a good quality of sprouts clean and at their best, they need picking over every three weeks all the autumn and winter, starting picking at the bottom of the stem and working up to the top.

In the 'twenties sprouts were picked into hampers of forty pounds each or potato sacks of forty pounds each. In the late 'twenties a breakthrough came in sprout packing. Mr Nicklen brought a truck load of old fish netting from Lowestoft which his women land workers cut into rectangular pieces. These were distributed around the village for folk to make sack shaped nets to hold twenty pounds of sprouts. A cottage industry was born which only lasted for two years, until the Bridport net makers cottoned on to the idea and began mass production of sprout nets.

PEAS

Another main crop grown on the farms was peas. I led a two-legged drill pulled by one horse up and down the pea field with George or Ralph holding the handles of the drill. We planted Early Bird, Telegraph, British Lion, Meteor varieties – all round-seeded peas – in February when the land was dry enough.

I liked pea drilling in February when the weak rays of the sun made the land disturbed by the drill steam; a boy with the harrows followed our work, covering the seed from the crows. An old saying I heard then when the amount of seed drilled was heavy in those early months of the year: 'One for the pigeon, one for the crow, one to rot, the other to grow.'

The land is cold in February and germination is slow. These peas would hopefully be fit to pick in early June.

We planted peas in rotation all the spring. The wrinkled seed were later varieties. No wrinkled seed was drilled until late March. These well known sorts of peas – Lincolns, Senators, Onwards, Duplex – were picked in July and August.

MANGOLDS

The stubble of the fallow land was heavily dressed with farmyard manure in the autumn and ploughed in before Christmas ready for mangold planting in March. Here again, a two legged drill fed the seed, which resembles Grape Nuts, down the spouts to the feet of the drill and planted it about two inches under the soil.

We grew about seven acres of mangolds. A good crop was forty tons per acre. When the young plants came through, Kainet, a potassic fertilizer, was sown as a top dressing. Then they were horse hoed, hand hoed, until the time came for them to be singled out: a soul-destroying job in the June sun, chopping away most of the plants and leaving single ones a foot apart.

There was little more to be done until mangold pulling in late October. The roots had the green tops cut from them with a sharp knife and the massive roots were thrown into heaps. Every evening the heaps were covered with leaves to protect them from frost until they were hauled and put in a bury, a long heap along the headland, like a barrow.

The women loaded the carts which hauled the mangolds. I led the horse from field to bury where Ralph built this roof top shaped stack of roots. Covered by straw, hedge croppings, asparagus bower, mouldy hay, and finally with earth, the mangolds stayed undisturbed until Christmas when they were used as feed, all the time gaining sugar as they matured. It's often been said that growing mangolds is a dear way to cart water about. True, they do contain a high proportion of water. Cattle like them pulped, sheep like them whole, and horses do in moderation. I reckon that when stock have had dry food all winter and the grass is late coming in spring, mangolds are a tonic, something juicy and sweet.

CHAPTER THREE

Improvements

It was a cold March morning when Ernest Roberts drove his car into our yard to accompany Dad on a rare visit to London. Mr Roberts was a sort of local Billy Morris, a quiet, pipe-smoking engineer from Grafton. He was essentially a farmer, but his heart was in machinery. He was the only man who could make the wheels go round on the barn engine which drove our chaff cutter and mangold pulper.

They set off from Ashton station and took the G.W.R. London train at Evesham.

Mother told us that if the Sunbeam car at London car mart was right and straight for Mr Roberts, Dad would buy it.

'What about Polly and the governess car?' I asked her.

Mother could not, or would not answer my questions. She just smiled. There were already three cars in the village and Mother looked forward to Dad's being number four. She was not interested in horses, but I loved Polly the liver chestnut mare, and journeys to market or shopping.

Dad already had a 1917 Fordson tractor which relieved Ralph of some of the ploughing. With his cap turned back to front and wearing goggles, he drove up and down the clay furrows with George sitting on the plough operating the levers at the headland. More often than not the tractor was in the barn, with Ernest

109

Thou great inventor, Henry Ford!

Roberts lying on a wheat sack repairing its innards; or he and Dad would be in the workshop taking the magneto to pieces after it had spent an hour or two in the oven of the kitchen grate drying out. Tractors were somewhat unreliable machines; Ralph and the older men were dubious of their possibilities. Rain or shine, the four-horse team in front of Ralph turned the furrows slowly but surely. It had always been the same, as Ralph said, 'Since before the remembrance of man.'

It was twilight when the Sunbeam came into our yard. It only stayed a few minutes for Ernest Roberts had a home for it under the thatch of his barn as he had to do 'just a few little adjustments' to it. I caught a glimpse of the grey open tourer with black mudguards and Dad followed Mr Roberts's car the mile and a half to Grafton. He came back soon after just before my bedtime and sat opposite the Grafton engineer over a cup of tea. 'I reached thirty miles an hour from Broadway, Lily,' Dad said proudly to Mother. 'That's right, isn't it, Ernest?' he added.

Mr Roberts's face never altered from the eternal smile. He nodded and said, 'Tom will be alright. He drove all the way from Chipping Norton.'

The next morning being Saturday, my brother Tom and I walked to Grafton after breakfast and took a look at our new transport in morning light. Sitting on the leather covered horse-hair driving seat the Klaxon horn was a new toy for me. Pressing the knob, the sound was impatient. Mr Roberts had the bonnet raised and was looking at the engine like a dentist searching for a decayed tooth. He never spoke, for his mind was on more important things than Klaxon horns.

The following Saturday we walked to Grafton, Mother, Tom and me, with Dad to take us for what he called 'a spin'. Mother sat beside Dad in front with Tom and me in the back. Up Stanway Hill to Stow-on-the-Wold with the hood down and no side screens but a glass partition with a leather apron to protect us from the cold wind. What a wind. The cold was cutting like a knife and I thought of peaceful drives behind Polly in the governess car. This new experience soon made it plain to Mother that the boys needed scarves, overcoats and gloves for further spins in the car.

I wondered why the motor had to stay at Grafton, but the following week Jack Hunting, our rough carpenter, arrived with

Sixteen horse power

a bag of tools and partitioned off one of the stables and made a great opening through the wattle and daub walls to the road. He made two doors for what was to be known as 'the motor house'. No fancy name like garage. The doors were painted with white panels and black imitation beams where the wattle and daub had been. Conservation was an uncoined word but it was decided that these half-timbered looking doors would at least match the rest of the house.

Here in the motor house between two mangers and hay racks the car took over where four horses had been stabled under the hay tallet (loft). There were ample stables for the working horses but Min and Tommy who took turns to pull the milk float were to be housed next door behind the partition wall.

The old stable lost the smell of generations of horses. The manger where the baited horses had snorted over their corn and chaff became the tool box where the car jack, the drum of lubricating oil and the two gallon cans of petrol marked Pratts were stored. The only Pratts I knew before then were Ralph Pratt the carter and his son Frank, my friend. When the car's long starting handle was turned and sixteen horses, or horse power came to life, the fumes from the exhaust stained Jack Hunting's creation, the pseudo Tudor doors, with a black patch, oily and smelly.

The Friday morning journeys to Evesham to do the shopping and to the bank took a little less than fifteen minutes, while Polly and the governess car had taken half an hour owing to the steep hill called Sedgeberrow Bank. The cobbled square in front of the Kings Head where little boys held farmers' horses while their owners did business in town were now sparsely covered with what relatively was the 'New Invention', the motor car.

That year Dad looked after his car, tended it like a baby, polished the brass headlights and used Cherry Blossom boot polish to clean and polish the mudguards. He had bought a pair of Wellington boots for this weekly exercise, the first pair I had seen, for everyone, master and man, wore the heavy hobnailed boots on the land and leggings in winter. It's true some did put on galoshes over their shoes in bad weather, but they were for children and ladies. From the brass tap over the horse trough Dad connected what he called a 'hoose' pipe, a rubber hose, and with a brush cleaned the grey body of the Sunbeam.

WIRES AND WIRELESS

Those who lived among the fruit and vegetable plantations of the Evesham Vale communicated with the cities by telegram from the Midland Station on the branch line. Some days Dad's desk was cluttered up with buff envelopes, little legends, brief notes from the city merchants. Reading these was like studying form at the races, or the stock market.

'LOAD SIXTY POTS OF SPROUTS TODAY, TRADE IMPROVING. CURNOW, NOTTINGHAM.'

– a typical wire, as they were known.

'NO MORE PLUMS PLEASE MARKET GLUTTED. HIPPENSTALL, HALIFAX.'

Another would come just as George had a load on the dray on his way to the station, only to be turned back.

Then the private wires came, ominous messages of death, and sometimes tidings of birth:

'POOR JIM KILLED BY THE GLOUCESTER EXPRESS GOODS. DO PLEASE COME TOM. LOVE EMMA.'

Jim Brase, a guard on the railway, had lived at Derby and was a favourite brother-in-law of Dad's.

'CARRIE AND I HAVE A BABY DAUGHTER,
KATHLEEN. LOVE TO UNCLE TOM AND AUNT LILY.'

Dad looked grave and asked me please to keep quiet for a while
when from Tipton the word came:

'YOUR BROTHER BILL NOT EXPECTED TO LAST
MORE THAN A WEEK.'

These were all incoming messages. Some had to have their
answer, so the half mile Groaten Lane to the station was a regular
run for me with wires to the booking office until Dad bought me
an eighteen-inch frame bike from Williams of Cheltenham. It was
at the booking office I stood by Ray Priday the porter who
courted cousin Mary and watched the messages tapped out in
morse code. The incoming wires were recognized by the buzzing
noise on the panel. He ignored the messages to other stations on
the line but when the words were tapped out for Ashton he wrote
down the message on a paper marked 'telegram'. The computer
of 1924 was a mahogany wooden box by the stove in the booking
office.

But things were changing fast; the Parish Council applied to
the Post Office for the telephone to be brought to our village. Mr
J.C. Nicklen, who almost worshipped every stick and stone of
the parish, was doubtful. He didn't like the thought of poles and
wires altering the ancient form of the village street. Mr Hughes
the artist who chaired the council was undecided for he didn't
want the canvas of field hedgerow to be marred by the intrusion.
However, the phone came. Our number was four and the initial
subscriber's number ten, and he was Policeman Smith. We had an
extension to Mr Bailey's farm, Dad's partner. By winding a
handle he was available at all times. Speaking to him half a mile
away was a new experience, my first phone call.

'What do you think of it, Fred?' he asked.

Words failed me, but I just said after a pause, 'Hallo, Mr
Bailey, are you well?'

What a boon it became, for Mr Bailey and Dad would talk for
two hours in an evening and plan the crops, decide on ploughing,
mowing, harvesting, while every morning they plotted the jobs
for the men at half past six before they arrived for work at seven.

George to horse hoe the peas, the shepherd to sort out twenty fat lambs for Bert to take on the dray to market. You see Mr Bailey was always up very early in the morning and he had already had a sniff at the weather. He'd probably been on Bredon Hill with his gun and assessed the morning soil. Last night's conditions might have been quite different.

The telephone poles soon became unnoticed except by Mr Hughes and Mr Brice, both artists of the landscape. Mrs Vale ran in circles around our kitchen every time the telephone bell rang. 'Mrs Archer, the telebell is ringing, the telebell,' then Mrs Vale escaped to her haunt in the back kitchen.

Ashton 204

In the sprout season Dad would ring Jim Curnow the fruit and vegetable merchant of Nottingham and be told how much the pots of sprouts had realized in the early morning market. Telegrams from Nottingham became unnecessary, instant prices came over the wires through Mr and Mrs Tandy at the exchange. To them it meant longer days in the Post Office to take early morning and late night calls. No morse code, no dreaded buff coloured envelopes. Even the postman came on a motor bike with panniers instead of a horse-drawn cart.

Sammy Grove descended from a family of market gardeners, but, like Ernest Roberts the Grafton engineer, left the land. He ran a fleet of three steamboats on the Avon: the *Diamond Queen*, the *Lilybird* and one whose name escapes me. One he steamed through canals and locks to his wharf next to the rowing club. Singing from the trippers accompanied by a piano gave Evesham music which could be heard as far away as the Abbey Bell Tower. Sammy was a musical man, a member of an old Evesham Light Orchestra. When he opened his music shop near the Town Hall it became a mecca for the gramophone addicts of the day. It was here that some village folk bought the records of popular tunes. Always thinking of the future, he toyed with the idea of building and selling wireless sets, crystal sets, valve sets. Maybe it was an advertising stunt when he decided to give a wireless concert in our Recreation Room.

The morning he arrived with his wireless several village folk were employed in the preparations. It so happened that Dad and his partner Mr Bailey had bought at a farm sale a load of sawn larch poles suitable for ladder-making. They were wired together in pairs and lay in our barn. Jack Hunting had made rungs for the ladders out of red withy in his workshop, and drilled holes in the poles; the fruit-picking ladders ranged from fifteen to forty rungs. I watched him by lantern light on winter evenings forming the rungs with a draw knife and spoke shave and fit it all together.

'I shall want a long pole for an aerial, Tom,' Sammy said as he stood in our yard. One of the younger farm workers wired a larch pole to the gable end of our barn. Sammy had twisted and stapled the end of a long copper wire to the pole with two shining white porcelain insulators, a foot apart and a yard from the pole. The reel of copper wire was played out long enough to reach Mr Nicklen's walnut tree. Here it was fastened and two insulators put in position. From the long aerial another length of copper wire led to the Recreation Room. Jack Hunting bored a hole with brace and bit while Sammy inserted an insulated sleeve to act as conduit to the wireless set.

It was Saturday morning and with other boys we just stood agog looking at the mast-like erection. Jack Hunting then dug a hole with a grafting tool just outside the Recreation Room in Mr

Nicklin's orchard. It appeared like an outsize post hole.

'We want an old bucket, Tom,' Sammy said to Dad. From the cooling house by the cowshed an old milk bucket, one that leaked, was dropped into the hole. Sammy soldered a copper wire to the bucket, an earth wire, but before Jack was allowed to bury it, he insisted that two buckets of water were poured in. Water, he said, would make a better earth.

Six o'clock the posters read on the shed by the cross and at the top of Blacksmiths Lane: the concert would begin at six o'clock. The Recreation Room held one hundred people in comfort, but that Saturday night it was bursting at the seams. Old folk who had not left the fireside for years came; school children came; in fact everyone was there, except a few who said it was the 'work of the devil', while one man said it would upset the weather as it happened every year the clocks were altered.

Hardly anyone had listened in before, but some months previously I had gone with my brother Tom to Ray Priday's cottage where he had a crystal set. He had taken the headphones apart so that both of us could hear Big Ben strike six o'clock.

At six o'clock on the night of the concert Sammy Grove's three-valve set connected to a horn loudspeaker rang out those notes loud and clear. I sat with my friend Frank by the coke stove and overheard one man say, 'It can't be from London 'cos it's a job to hear the church clock at Beckford if the wind isn't in the right quarter.' Peter Eckersley was the announcer who introduced John Henry and Blossom in a comic sketch. The silence in the hall could be felt, it was as if something had arrived amongst us from the stars above. Shepherd Tidmarsh chuckled, puffing at his clay pipe. He had an ability to catch a joke almost before the punchline.

Then we had music and song. The horn loudspeaker crackled like the breaking of firesticks, it whistled and hooted. The audience laughed as Sammy played with the two coils, opening them and closing them like a nut cracker. The music and song was superior to that from any of Sammy's gramophone records. Charlie Nicklin thanked Sammy Grove for the concert and he remarked, 'I knew it was to be a wireless concert when I saw the wires from Tom Archer's barn.' Village folk grouped around the trestle table where the valves from the batteries glowed, and wondered. They stood like women round the pram of a newborn child. Shepherd Tidmarsh walked around the back. I gathered he was dubious, wondering whether the sound came from a record.

Some little time after, when Ernest Roberts had made a wireless for himself, he began making them for sale. Our family was invited to a wireless evening at his house and Dad bought a set from him, a three-valve set which was linked to the aerial on the barn, then to a chimney. Another milk bucket was buried for the earth wire. Every evening Dad twiddled the knob on the coils and we could choose our programme, 5XX from Daventry or 2LO from London. The wireless dulled the blow for us all of the loss of the milking herd. Our set with HT and LT batteries had a selection of coils to fit on the set. Dad liked to twiddle them and get foreign stations. After tea Peter Eckersley announced, 'This is 2LO calling, 2LO calling,' and we heard Big Ben from London.

The programmes were essentially entertainment after the news. John Henry and Blossom, a comedy; Stainless Stephen, who recited his pieces of jokes about himself. He called himself Stainless Brainless Stephen. Nosmo King, Leonard Henry. Dad liked Mabel Constanduras and 'Grandma', an early family saga: Grandma was always putting the damper on everything. Jack Payne's dance band, Trose and his Mandoleers. At Christmas, Bransbry Williams as Scrooge from Dickens's *Christmas Carol* was so real, Bob Cratchit so sad a character. Bransbry Williams's interpretation of the ghost of Christmas past was the first real ghost story I heard over the wireless waves.

The two penny [1p] *Radio Times* was scrutinized every week; the legend read, 'What are the wild waves saying.' I remember a broadcast one Halloween called 'The Eve Of All Souls', after which taking the candle up the stairs to bed was quite frightening.

We had a long lead on the horn loudspeaker Sunday summer nights on the lawn. Shepherd Tidmarsh and his wife sat there on the garden wall to hear programmes which had to have a religious flavour. One Sunday morning Dad twiddled the coils and got the first radio ham I had heard. His voice came from Harvington near Evesham. Dad said to Mother, 'Lily, the air's full of it, full of it.'

Later the 1926 Wembley Exhibition was broadcast. Gypsy Smith sang one Sunday, 'What A Friend We Have In Jesus'. Dad thought that wonderful. 'Children's Hours' with Uncle Mac when birthdays were read out and if it was twins, the voice came loud and clear, 'Hallo, twins.'

Mr Bailey had some earphones for his set and went to sleep with them on only to be wakened by a loud soprano singing in his ears. He was always well up on the weather forecasts, but Shepherd Tidmarsh never believed in them. He had always prophesied the weather without it coming from London.

THE SEPTIC TANK

Mother's brother, Frank, was a builder from Knowle near Birmingham. It happened that work was slack so he came and put in a modern convenience. Jack Hunting dug the hole for the septic tank and Uncle Frank put in the sewer pipe from outside the workshop to the tank next to the privy under the nut bushes: a flush job, inspection pits, the lot, with a WC in the bedroom converted to bathroom. Pulling the chain was great fun but Dad said, 'You boys must still go to the privy up the garden and keep the WC for emergencies.' I don't think we kept strictly to that rule.

A big iron Beeston boiler fitted in the back kitchen with inch and a half pipes to the bathroom gave us hot water to the new bath. We had an airing cupboard, the woodwork painted brown by Mr Higgins, the blacksmith's carpenter; it was a kind of waggon paint that never dried. That was a problem, but we were now one of the few with a WC and bath.

THE NEW ROOM AT STANLEY FARM

On the right of the hall, known as the passage, a dark cellar-like room with a tiny window and an earth floor had been used as a coal house and wood store. Here through the open window which gave only a chink of light even in summer, fourteen cats came to and fro from the barns and yard at will. Cats which were half wild, and lived on what they could hunt: birds, mice, rats; they were given a daily drink of warm milk from the cows in the lid of a seventeen gallon milk churn. The eeriness of the place combined with a feel of the past, a time when Stanley Farm was unoccupied for years, being considered by the old folk as a haunted house.

When a new litter of kittens were born in the wood pile I ventured in by candlelight. Creeping up to the she cat, the light of the candle started her spitting and making noises which sounded so much like 'jam roll'. I warily put a saucer of milk at a safe distance from the mother and her kittens. Multi-coloured cats, black and white, ginger, claimed their den as no doubt they and their ancestors had done for years. Bats hung like faded leaves from the cobwebbed high ceiling. The smell of the place was of rats, damp, old timber, fire logs, and earth. A big black Tom cat we called Nigger would jump from the window ledge and try and steal the milk from the new brood of kittens.

There was something very primitive about these wild cats. They could never be handled. They hunted in the corn ricks for vermin at night, but came in, a little caravan of tigers, after their milk in the cowshed every morning when the cows were turned out to grass.

Jack Hunting, that little bent man who was known as a rough carpenter, came infrequently to the old coal house to control the population of cats. I was fond of old Jack, for in a way he was like Grandad, but he was a real rustic, a village oracle. Gentle with children, yet he had no scruples with cats. An Irish Terrier named Rough followed him everywhere at work and to the pub, where, when things went wrong at his sister-in-law's, where he lodged, he had what was known as 'a session'. For a week he might be befuddled with cider.

Jack, wearing a thick pair of hedging gloves, unafraid of the she cat, would gather her brood of kittens into a sack and walk up the churchyard with a brick under his arm, then drown the kittens in the moat pond with the brick in the sack with his quarry. I only followed him once on his mission and wondered why this awful waste of life could be really the only answer to the ever-increasing number of cats on the farm.

He caught Nigger the big Tom one summer day and was about to doctor him in the rickyard by the barn door, but Nigger escaped and was never seen again. Maybe he joined another tribe, because tribes there were in all the farmyards under the hill.

Soon after the coal house was to become a new and grand drawing room. Jack came with his frail basket of tools, carried as always on his back by sliding his seven pound axe through the webbing handles and suspending his basket on the axe helve or handle with the sharp head at the back of his left shoulder. The half timbered wall was measured for the rough carpenter to make a hole just big enough to take the frame of a bay window. Watching him saw through the beams gave me a curious sense of change. I realized that the den would be no more, not for the cats, the bats, for games of hide-and-seek.

The hole in the wall revealed something no one had ever seen. The light from the orchard across the road shone in and showed the primitive construction of the room. The huge beams above where the bats hung were so massive, white with age and pegged together, numbered with Roman numerals, a cathedral in miniature, open to the thatched roof. It was like the draining of a river bed or the emptying of a well – all was revealed which before had been seen by only candlelight. The cats on the wood pile spat, grumbled and growled, but stayed awhile until Jack carved another hole for a window to open into the yard. That was too much. They fled first of all to the gaps under the manger in the cowshed, then they took over the granary where great wooden bins made little private rooms for the summer vagrant pea pickers and were filled with oats every autumn. This was a cat's haven. Sparrows, when they came hungry through the window for grain, were easy prey. They stood no chance.

After Jack Hunting had let the daylight into the old coal house, Ralph the carter backed a muck cart up to the opening and men worked all day moving the coal and wood and then dug up the earth floor to be scattered, black with the remains of decades of coal onto the grassland of Church Close. Jack then laid concrete a foot deep as a foundation for what was to be a parquet floor.

Every day home from school I watched the progress on the room. If it rained Dad put men to work helping Jack shovelling and mixing, but Jack remained in charge. He built a chimney breast wide enough to take a big fireplace, then he cut his way through the thatched roof and built a chimney and joined its three fellow chimneys from the house, the dining room, and the back kitchen. I never saw the four chimneys all puffing smoke together, they took their turn: the back kitchen on wash days, the dining room on Sundays. I wondered when the drawing room fire would be burning, but was fairly sure it would be Christmas, birthdays or when someone came who looked important for the evening.

Jack fixed the ceiling, the bare rafters over a couple of big beams all ready for the lath and plaster. Jack was not to plaster the ceiling, this was a skilled job to be done by Sapper Haines, ex-Engineers, of Enfield Cottage.

Sapper was an artist in plaster. A stocky man, he had a swagger walk and smoked a cherry wood pipe – a big pipe which would hold getting on for an ounce of tobacco. Sapper liked his cider and when I started at the grammar school at ten years old and had a spattering of French from Mademoiselle Oppenheim, Sapper talked to me in pigeon French when his tongue had been loosened with cider. I was supposed to answer, but the little I knew was too unlike Sapper's lingo.

When the time came for the plastering, Jack's job was to prepare the mixture after he had nailed the laths to the rafters. Two sacks of cow hair came, I believe, originally from the Argentine. The hair had to be beaten with lath sticks until it was fluffy and soft to go into Sapper's lime plaster. Up in the tallet or loft over the motor house, Jack hammered away at the cow hair raising a dust storm of dried grease and perhaps germs – there could easily have been anthrax or the dreaded foot and mouth disease. It was just common practice of the day to use cow hair to bind the plaster. Sapper ran the putty, as he called it, just slaking lump lime until it was like a putty. What else he used in the mixture I don't know, but the cow hair was all put in the mixing barrel.

The summer holidays from school had been so hot that the men in the hayfield were close behind Ralph's mowing machine. Hay was made the next day after the mowing. Tom Whittle our cowman was busy building the rick and I was sent to Ten Furlongs field for the cows, cows which suckled calves and just one to be milked for the house. As I turned the corner from Gypsies Lane into the Groaten I followed the cows, imitating Tom the cowman, propelled by an ash plant, and there with a bucket stood Jack Hunting. 'Hy, Master Frederick. I want some cow muck, fresh and warm.'

I looked at him and said, 'For the celery trench, ay?'

'No, for parge,' he replied, 'I'm g'wain to parge yer Dad's new chimney.'

First one cow then another obliged as the cow pats from the grass fed animals fell on the brick floor of the cowshed. Jack filled his bucket and went away.

Following Jack to the building work, I watched him mix the cow manure with lime mortar, and plaster it on the inside of the chimney from the bottom as far as he could reach. He had plastered the upper part of the chimney with ordinary mortar, but parge, that mixture of antiquity, was the answer for the lower part to prevent the fire from cracking the mortar.

Sapper made his usual perfect job of the ceilings and walls. Jack fixed picture rails, while Dad insisted on chair rails as well. The room with the bay window, window seat and two little windows overlooking the yard would soon be colour washed with different colours above and below the chair rails.

One morning Mr Garland came over from Grafton on a motor bike. He was to instruct Dad in the art of parquet flooring. The oak blocks had been delivered, the pitch and tar was boiling in a barrel over a fire in the yard. Jack became labourer. He carried the boiling mixture of pitch and tar in a bucket, and spread it thinly on the concrete floor and Mr Garland, starting in the middle of the room, made a huge jigsaw puzzle of oakwood blocks. Then Dad took over and under Mr Garland's eye continued the jigsaw.

'Now when you finish, Tom, you must have a border of blocks running alongside the wall so that the little pieces needed to infill the pattern are not next the wall.'

So I watched Dad form what I called the headland, a narrow path of blocks side by side, three or four wide, for wasn't it just like ploughing an awkward shaped field when the horses turned on the headland and the carters had their bait on the headland and that was ploughed last of all to finish the field?

The room was almost complete, painted green below the chair rails and cream above with a whiter than white ceiling, the work of Sapper, and now a wooden framed fireplace with tiles up either side covered in wild flowers. Whether I liked it or not was none of my business, but I did wonder why we needed another room, for the dining room was not used every day. It's true the fire smoked in the dining room, but not until Harry Attwood swept it and left his brush up the chimney. That had been retrieved and returned. Harry was more amused than Dad.

Now for furniture. A moquette three-piece suite came from Birmingham and a dining table and chairs just in case we were to have tea in there, for the room was twice the size of the dining room. Among Dad's many friends one I thought was not his type. He was a dealer, a dealer in anything: fruit and veg., furniture, bankrupt stock. His name, Shatherum Walker. I reckon he was of Jewish extraction. He had tiny little black curls of hair which crowned his broad head like the hair springs from a pocket watch. They were jet black, the features around the hook shaped nose were well fleshed and two piercing blue eyes made him a man with a face of great character. I never spoke to him, he was much too grand.

He arrived one day at Stanley Farm driving a Ford car packed with rugs, furs and carpet. Supposedly he'd been to Russia. That was questionable. But here was a man with a flair for selling, a man of the marketplace with the gift of persuasion. 'Now, Tom, here's some floor covering for your drawing room you told me about in Evesham Market.'

He rolled out an Indian carpet which would cover half the room, golden and red patterned like a landscape of mountain and flood.

'I wouldn't sell it to anyone, but to you it's a tenner.'

Dad looked at it, Mother craved for it, and I thought it beautiful. After a moment's hesitation Shatherum Walker threw a fur coat across the settee and said, 'Try that for size, Mrs Archer.'

Mother slipped it on, walked to the mirror in the hall and fancied herself, and why not I thought. After naming several arctic fur-bearing animals, Shatherum admitted it was some kind of coney.

'Take the two, the carpet and the coat, twenty quid.'

Mother gave Dad one of those disarming looks hard to ignore. He nodded assent, but the dealing had not finished. 'How about a hearth rug Tom, Rangoon tails.'

The rug just fitted in front of the hearth and sure enough it was made out of the tails of some animal of the tiger tribe. He threw in another mat he called opossum, and Dad, after a bit of haggling, wrote the cheque. The cats had left the den, to be replaced by more of the cat tribe under foot, and Mother had a fur coat.

'It is really rabbit skin, Mother,' I said as I fingered the moth ball smelling fur.

'Coney they call it, sounds better,' she replied.

With the china cabinet moved from the dining room holding the few family heirlooms, a black ebony leaded light piece, one thing was missing for a drawing room, a piano. Dad lived his life in four places: on the land, at home, at market, and farm sales. No cottage piano from the famous firm in Cheltenham's Promenade would take his eye. A sale at some country mansion and an out-of-tune grand piano was knocked down to Dad for five pounds. The mahogany top was beautiful when it arrived with Ralph the carter on the dray. Two or three men coaxed it into position in the corner by the window. I opened the lid and saw the rows of ivories all complete but different from our piano in the house place. The black was still black, yet the supposedly white ivory keys reminded me of tobacco stained teeth, yellow, aged and dull.

Mother had the piano tuner to call and it was soon shipshape. She fancied playing the grand, while the upright was my brother's province when he had lessons with Miss Morris in the evenings.

Mr Garland came again, vetted the parquet floor and said it was alright. He was courting an Ashton lady and it was common knowledge that they were to marry. Mother congratulated him but he was so shy he blushed the colour of geraniums then whispered, 'Thank you.'

'Tom,' he said, 'your drawing room door. I could grain it for you, it would look better.'

'Alright then, George, I'll leave it to you,' Dad replied.

Mr Garland came next day with paint combs and graining instruments. He painted the door yellow and next day when the paint had dried he coated it with a brown paint. While this was still wet he conjured with the combs and made false knots in the wood with his tools showing the knots as yellow flaws in the wood from the undercoat, a sort of pseudo antique oak door made of pine wood. It pleased everyone at the time, but I wondered why the grain and the knots had to be there at all.

The oil lamp in the house place, brass and polished, trimmed and filled daily by Mrs Vale, was old, the light it gave was yellow. One Saturday Dad returned from Gloucester Market in the car with a cardboard box. 'What is it?' I enquired, but Mother knew what he was buying that day.

'An Aladdin lamp,' he replied, as he took the chromium-plated bowl and the glass globe from the box. Another box held the delicate mantles. In no time at all it hung from the ceiling, shedding a white incandescent light to every corner of the room.

So by the fire and sitting on the Rangoon tails rug we spent an evening in a light which had never before shone in Stanley Farm. Dad carried the loudspeaker from the wireless set in the house place on a long flex and put it on the table. The first night in the drawing room – the cat den had become Aladdin's cave.

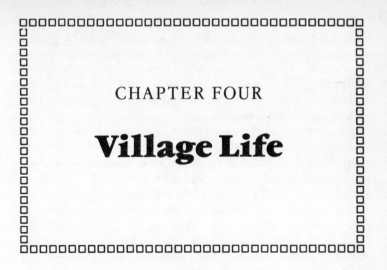

CHAPTER FOUR

Village Life

Before the telephone and wireless came to broaden the horizons of villagers beyond the nearby Cotswolds and Malvern hills, which sometimes looked so near that the houses on the hillside could be seen, sometimes a distant misty mound far away, village life was self-sufficient, cosily independent from town.

Charlie Moore made ladders for ricks and fruit picking, he made hurdles for the sheep fold, making a dozen hurdles a day from the withy poles pollarded every seven years, a product of the trees lining Carrants Brook. His artistry in green wood watched by village children was also an education. He was just one of many folk who practised their craft in the parish, using tools unaltered since the remembrance of the oldest villager. His simple workshop contained a honed drawknife and a cleaver, the knife which he twisted to split the poles until the half rounded rails were ready to make the gate-like hurdles of Gloucestershire. His ladders were made from sawn half-rounded larch poles, then the rungs fitted in red withy, a tough sort of willow. Sometimes he used sally or sallow for the rungs, from the stool-grown pussy willow stumps from the coppices. He made light ladders for fruit picking, forty-rung ladders for the high pear trees and for picking the green pickling walnuts which had to be gathered before August Bank Holiday when the nuts became woody. Everything was done according to the old traditions of craft work. Charlie umpired village cricket matches on Saturdays and read from a Bible the size of a stable door under the walnut tree on Sunday afternoons.

Village life consisted of long hours of work for a meagre financial reward, but the satisfaction of a job well done. The baker, Mr Hugh Clements, turned out his artistry in dough: four pound loaves, cottage loaves, taken from the oven in the bakehouse at the rear of his house daily with that long handled shovel-like tool called a 'peel'. He made currant loaves, milk loaves, currant cakes, wholesome and filling.

In the bread oven cottagers' Sunday joints were cooked on special occasions when the tiny cottage range ovens were too small to take the joints. With a two-wheeled sprung baker's cart Mr Clements delivered daily bread, cakes for the family, sharps or middlings for the cottagers' pigs, maize for poultry. Mr

A harvest of withies

Clements had a fast cob named Express which could do the six miles to Evesham in twenty-four minutes. This daily delivery of bread was one of the mainsprings of community life. But Mr Clements was not only a baker, he was also a farmer: he was a real all-rounder. The world has changed so much for now we live in a nation of specialists where the complete all-rounder is rare. It used to be said that Hugh Clements was involved in every trade except that of a coal merchant. Mrs Clements, a busy little body, was always at work. She was a lady of the back room and she also kept the Post Office. Mr Clements's parents had kept the Plough and Harrow Inn long before my time and for a while Hugh Clements and his son were landlords of the Star. On Little Hill by the Cuckoo Pen a small flock of his sheep bred lambs every year for market.

Hugh Clements's house was surrounded with orchards where he grew apples and plums, his cider from the gnarled old trees was quite special. He had no trouble getting casual labour for haymaking. Men who had worked fifty-two hours in other fields would help him after tea getting in the hay, the cider being an extra bonus on top of the overtime money.

Not only did he sell his own fruit, he bought fruit at auction. He seemed to love a gamble; a real gamble when the prices at market for apples were so uncertain.

Mr Clements was possibly the earliest riser in the parish, for his bread baking started about four o'clock in the morning and the hot loaves were loaded into the baker's cart for early delivery. His man Bill Henning milked his twelve cows starting at five o'clock, then Mr Clements did his round with the milk while his son delivered the bread. At one time the milk was delivered with a shoulder yoke and two buckets to be dipped out with pint and quart measures into the jugs and basins waiting on the door steps, then came a gleaming copper churn on wheels with a tap at the bottom like a giant tea urn. He tapped the cooled fresh milk into a three gallon bucket and walked briskly from cottage to cottage dispensing his two pence a pint creamy liquor from his Shorthorn herd. Mrs Clements would be up early making butter, selling bread and butter at the door.

Mr Clements also made very special cider. At autumnal cider-making he made enough cider to satisfy his cowman, his casual haymakers and family friends; the footballers refreshed

Yokes for the cowman

themselves with it after matches, Shepherd Tidmarsh when the shearing of his sheep in June was on his calendar, Tom Whittle would call and be refreshed after he had advised Mr Clements on drenching a sick cow. Stodge Warren the roadman swilled down his bread and cheese lunch with it as he rested awhile in his barrow in the village street from the regular grind of siding or edging the roadside verges with stock axe and shovel, or cutting the waist-high hemlock from the roadside with his scythe in high summer.

After midday dinner Mr Clements would tend his small flock of sheep up on the hill by the Cuckoo Pen, or pick his orchards of fruit with Bill Henning his cowman and his son Hugh.

Behind the brick-built house with the legend 1895 over the gable was the bake house. The Clements were a typical yeoman family of one hundred acres who helped the poor at Christmas and arranged a whist drive for a young man who was ill with pneumonia.

A typical countryman in the 'twenties was our carter Ralph. What was his life, his day, his work, his budget? Ralph earned thirty-four shillings [£1.70] a week, the four shillings extra to the standard thirty was because he worked fifty-four hours looking after his horses, feeding them early in the morning, late at night. In summer Ralph earned some overtime money at nine pence an hour.

He rose at four o'clock, ate a little breakfast by candlelight, then walked a quarter of a mile from Paris on the hillside to Boss Close where his seven horses grazed. He drove them all to the stable at Old Manor Farm and tied them to their mangers where they had what he called a dew-bit, a piece of bread and something while the dew was still on the grass, then had half an hour pulling the sweet clover hay from their racks. Then he geared up his two horses for the mowing machine and by five o'clock he was circling the mowing grass with his machine (see p.94). At ten o'clock he had his bait or lunch: the top of a cottage loaf, a good piece of cheese, an onion and a bottle of lukewarm tea, under the shade of the hedgerow.

Ralph was a philosopher, a rural wit and sage. Here was Dogberry, the Shakespeare character in *Much Ado About Nothing*. To hear Ralph singing on the mower on mornings when most of the world lay on flock mattresses indicated that things were going what Arthur Street would call 'suently'. Of course he grumbled when the work went bad or if the weather was against him, but basically he was a happy man who came out with unexpected quips.

Ralph didn't enjoy the best of health but he soldiered on despite persistent eczema on his arms. He once told me after the doctor had prescribed one ointment after another that the old doctor was like 'an apple 'ooman'. His feet played him up, so he kept a selection of boots in the harness room with pieces cut out to ease his bunion, then he stuffed his boots with sheep's wool to ease his feet.

This spare little man had a backbone of true steel reinforced and encouraged by his good wife Clara. She was a good manager, a type of woman now extinct who could make a meal out of very little. Her family of four were well fed on wholesome food, lots of Mr Clements' bread, bacon from the pig. They were enormous cheese eaters. Clara made bread puddings which Ralph ate cold as a kind of afters with his bait.

Every year Ralph grew a ton of potatoes on some unco-operative headland. So at bait time, after discussing the horse work or Pleasant the mare's sore shoulders, the conversation turned to 'taters'. Taters were discussed from planting time to lifting time. No matter how William Cobbett had decried potatoes a hundred years before, declaring that bread was infinitely better, taters were a mainstay of Ralph and Clara's menu. Often have I been in their little cottage, perched as it was on the hillside, and seen the amount of potatoes and cabbage and fat bacon piled on dinner plates, wholesome and appetizing, or a rabbit stew with suety dumplings, hot and steaming on the table. A loaded supermarket trolley just could not provide the nutriment from Clara's kitchen. Hard times there were when potatoes were frosted but Ralph was rarely caught out for he kept his stable lantern lit with the wick turned down in the wash house where his sacks of yearly insurance were piled.

Pleasure for Ralph was his Sunday morning ringing of the tenor bell in the church, then a drink of cider with Tom Baldwyn at The Croft, his house; Tom sold cider in four and a half gallon barrels known as 'pins' for a few pence a gallon. Living on the hill, Ralph carried all his coal from the cart shed at Old Manor Farm, a hundredweight at a time, up a steep incline. Young Billy Drinkwater left it there for him, 'young' Billy being nearer sixty than fifty years old. Every night Ralph was burdened with a load of something or other. A frail basket full of bread, a can of paraffin, coal for the widow woman next door.

He went to the local flower shows some Saturday afternoons, and sang 'The Rose of Tralee' at village concerts. Christmas and New Year Ralph and the ringers sang carols around the houses. They rang the Old Year out and the half muffled peal told the world the year was gone, then the leather mufflers or buffs were taken off and all five bells were fired like the 1812 overture. The day after Ralph would say, 'I feel a bit washed out you. My yud aches, and what can I expect after all that homemade wine we had at Miss Bunch Baldwyn's.'

Years passed and Ralph, unable to do quite as much as when he was young said to me one day, 'I haven't done enough work today to satisfy myself, let alone the Gaffer.' The Gaffer (Dad) knew because he, like Ralph, had seen too many Christmas Days. Ralph then drew his Old Age Pension, the first money he had had from the State apart from a fortnight in Cheltenham hospital when the Panel Money was one pound a week.

In our village the question is often asked, where is the village centre? A place where the local news and gossip is exchanged. Long before the coffee morning, the WI wine and cheese party, labourers on the land, the railway and the roads met at the pub – a male province; women met at Mrs Cresswell's shop or Mr Tandy's post office, farmers at local markets, all social centres of the 1920s.

The fact was our pub had only beer and cider licences, anyone who drank spirits went farther afield. Walter Cresswell who kept The Star sold farm cider and local brewed ale. Albert Bell at The Plough and Harrow, a straw-thatched tavern with a big yard in front, did the same. His pub was a gem of a place with a big open fire, and an oil painting of two old workman ploughing and harrowing with the horses. Some liked Mr Cresswell's ale from Rowlands brewery in Evesham while others preferred Flowers ale from Stratford-on-Avon. I didn't know much of The Plough and Harrow but Mr and Mrs Walter Cresswell were near neighbours of ours. The place was clean and scrubbed. The floor

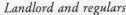

Landlord and regulars

was stone slabs off the hill, partly covered with coconut matting. The spittoon stood in the middle of the little bar parlour while the tobacco-chewing old gaffers of the land aimed as straight as a die at the sawdust filled iron contraption when they spat the surplus from their whiskered mouths.

When the cottagers reared large families with one bedroom and a landing to sleep in at night and the clothes-horse, laden with washing, hid the fire, men took a couple of hours away from it all at The Star. Often with sodden breeches and jackets, they steamed in front of a fire in that parlour, supped their ale, talked of crops, children's ponies, the weather and low wages. How the corduroys gave a scent mixed with shag and twist tobacco smoke in that oasis The Star.

Walter Cresswell was a quiet landlord, his wife a lovable God-fearing woman who came to Chapel. The semi-circular settle by the fireside was a haven for the locals while pea-pickers and gypsies sat outside on summer nights and sang. Over the bar the framed warning read:

> As a bird is known by his note
> So is a man known by his conversation.
> Swearing strictly prohibited.

Mrs Cresswell's hens strayed into our orchard and laid astray. When I returned her maybe a dozen eggs found in the stinging nettles, as her white Leghorn fowls ran back to her pen in the pub yard, she gave me a packet of biscuits and a bottle of pop and thanked me. In the garden in front of the pub, the drink house stood under a thatched roof to keep the beer cool in summer. It looked like a miniature cottage without a chimney, or an oversized dolls' house.

Mr Cresswell drove a nag and four-wheeled vehicle up and down the road to his field where he grew his acre of wheat, which was threshed in our rickyard when the machine came, and vegetables for his table. Walter ran the Sick and Dividend Christmas Club, which paid a little to any member who was ill, then the remainder was divided between the members at Christmas. It didn't pay to be ill early in the year because there was so little in the kitty then.

At Fred Tandy's shop folk collected their 'Lloyd George', as the pension was known. The window was decorated with jars of boiled sweets. Dad used to send me there with half a crown [12½p] for forty postage stamps, twenty penny and twenty halfpenny. A stuck down letter was three halfpence, a postcard one penny, while a tucked in envelope with printed matter one halfpenny. Every day I posted invoices to James Curnow, fruit and vegetable salesman of Nottingham; Heppenstalls of Bradford, Fergusons of Liverpool.

The printed carbon-copied letter book read 'Archer & Bailey'

Dear Sir,
This day we have sent you as follows:-

Then Dad just wrote:

40 pots (Hampers) of sprouts
or
50 pots of Warners King apples.

Easy book-keeping in those pre-computer days. Cheques came by post every week for the produce; and the cheque came the next day without fail from Messrs E.G. Righton & Son when we sent cattle or sheep to market. Envelopes addressed by Mr Righton's clerk were a picture in the thin-up-and-thick-down writing. Mr Fred Lewis was the clerk and Dad used to give me the envelope, saying, 'There's the way to write, you just copy Mr Lewis's writing.' I tried, but his writing was just artistry with a pen. I've never seen the like since then.

Fred Tandy's shop did a fair trade in Carter's tested seeds. The smallholders of Ayles Acre bought from him. We bought our mangold seed from his shop, but pea and bean seed from Mr Anderson, an wiry Irishman who travelled on his bike around the Vale for Watkins and Simson. In all weathers he came without overcoat or waistcoat, a man who rowed on the Avon in a crew which won many cups at Evesham Regatta – Evesham being known as the Henley of the Midlands.

Mrs Cresswell's shop had more variety as an emporium of village trade while Mr Tandy concentrated more on the post office, which he had taken over from Mr Clements. Mrs Cresswell, a lady who lost her husband in the '14 War, had on her shelves everything in the grocery line. Farm butter from Mr Clements, Brierley's ginger beer (a secret recipe invented by George Brierley of Evesham), homemade faggots and brawn, Red Bell tobacco at three pence halfpenny [1½p] for half an ounce, done up in cartridge shaped packets, cigarettes, clay pipes, candles, margarine, twopenny packets of cocoa. I liked to watch her slice the bacon with a sharp disc machine turned by a handle. No one wanted wafer-thin rashers and hers were fairly thick, good, wholesome and home-cured. A forty gallon drum of paraffin stood trammed like a beer barrel under the stairs with a tundish or funnel under the tap to fill the villagers' oil cans. She had a deft way of making a paper bag, shaped like an ice cream cornet, for sweets.

On hot summer days she made ice cream in a primitive machine. The handle turned the mixture in a jacket of ice and salt. Her cornets at a halfpenny each were custard coloured. The word went around the grapevine of the children at school, 'Mrs Cresswell's making ice cream today,' and soon the shop was full of boys and girls with their halfpennies. Mrs Cresswell used to sing at the concerts, a rural Florrie Ford when she sang, 'Don't Dilly Dally on the Way.' Trade at Mrs Cresswell's was a very necessary part of village life. Her first customers would buy their Woodbine cigarettes, Red Bell tobacco and chewing twist tobacco at 6.30 in the morning before they went to their field work. Most necessities of life could be found either at Mr Tandy's post office or Mrs Cresswell's shop, but three of four delivery vans came daily from somewhere afar to bring in the necessities to the village: a chain-driven Trojan van marked Brook Bond tea, another from D.C.L. yeast, and Wards of Evesham's early mobile shop selling paraffin, oil lamps, globes for oil lamps, candles, chamber pots, Eiffel Tower lemonade crystals, door mats. He was known simply as the oilman.

It would be wrong to assume that the village street was an empty narrow track when only three families had a car and the delivery vans were so few – it was a hive of activity. Early mornings in summer carters and plough boys rode their tandem teams side saddle to the hayfields. I see them with their heels dug into the horse's traces, with one hand on the reins, another holding the harness with the brass knobs which stood up as two slender arms six inches above the collars, and hear the clip clop of

Home from the field, sidesaddle

the massive Shires as they kicked up clouds of dust from the limestone, untarred road. One man with two strawberry roan geldings sat slouched as in an armchair puffing a Woodbine. A frail basket slung from the harness with a bottle peeping out, a bottle of cider or tea, and the eternal bread and cheese and fat bacon wrapped in last night's *Cheltenham Echo* tucked away ready for the ten o'clock bait. Intermittent convoys of men and animals going up and down to their work.

Arthritic Blenheim Allen propelled by an ash plant, driving his milking herd to the cowshed at Holloway Farm. A whiskered man in earth-coloured corduroys and a greasy hat, urging his cows along as they snatched mouthfuls of grass from the roadside verge and brushed the flies from their backs under the drooping ash tree by our house. He'd call at Brindy, always at the rear, 'Brindy, get on 'ull ya, I'll smite thee like Moses smote the rock when he was along of the children of Israel.' His cows toyed with him up the village street as if they knew he couldn't run after them and hurry them to their stalls.

In autumn, before the tractor, the aeroplane or the chain saw brought urban sounds to the countryside, the edge of night was the most magic time of day. Apart from a labouring goods train struggling up the incline, the sights and sounds of the village were of animals, birds and country folk: click clack of blackbirds making for their roosts in the hedges; cock up, cock up, from pheasants as they fluttered their wings to reach the top of the coppice trees; a newly calved cow calling for her calf; the folded sheep on the roots coughing – every cough followed by a fart. The metallic call of partridges settling for the night in the deep furrows of pasture where the lands were so deep that one could stand in one furrow and only see the head and shoulders of a friend in the next furrow. Some said the ancient formations of ridge and furrow of the claylands was made to make extra surface to a field, others said it was for drainage, while when the corn was cut before the pastures were laid down, the reaper with hook and crook hadn't to bend so low as he stood on the sideland cutting the corn towards the ridge. Starlings in their droves took the same course nightly from the feeding grounds of stubble and the windfall orchard apples to their roosts in the wood: a course like the flight path of aeroplanes of today, after they had stained some cottager's washing with their elderberry coloured droppings.

The homeward teams of horse and waggon from the harvest field as night fell in September: waggons creaked, horses snorted, their iron-shod hooves made sparks as they turned along the lane to the rickyard. The smell of tobacco from the carter's pipe and the twitter of a robin going late to its roost in the nut bushes, emerging to pick a late supper from the heaps of fresh hot khaki-coloured horse muck in the road.

The lantern-lit inn sign at The Star creaked comfortingly in the evening breeze; a dog barked from its cider-barrel kennel: a mist came along the brookside meadows and rabbits ventured from their burrows, clipping the clover on the headland; the horses ungeared and turned out into their field; the sound of the chog chain when the milk cows were untied from their mangers and squirted their loose dung on the cowshed floor as they left, as if they couldn't wait to manure the field.

The work day was over, except for the paper boy who delivered the *Echo* around the houses. Men went home to their evening meals, each carrying a piece of firewood on one shoulder, with an empty frail food basket as a satchel on their back. They scauted (scraped) the earth from their hobnailed feet before reaching the garden gate, making the sparks fly magnesium blue as they noisily lumbered home with tired limbs.

'Good night, Ralph.'

'Good night to you, Tom.'

'Might see you at The Star, or 'unt it a Whist Drive tonight?'

'No dall [damn], 'tis bell ringing practice.'

Some went to The Star while five men pulled the ropes at the belfry making music. Sometimes a buff peal saying farewell to an old ringer.

Sounds of lighter boots on the road at 7.30 and the chatter of women meant that their candle lanterns were showing them the way to the Recreation Room and whist. One familiar sound was Mr Bell's wooden leg pounding alongside his good one, a brave man from The Plough And Harrow who climbed fruit-picking ladders, rode a motor bike and did more with one leg than lots did with two. He walked beside Frank Whittle, who, on crutches since losing a leg in the war, took strides of over a yard, another one of the men of metal. He followed the hounds on crutches, walked miles at night over the hill to his favourite pub.

Then Edward the midnight milkman began his little round

with Lavender his cob in the milk float. Two hurricane lamps swung from the front of his two-wheeled vehicle. He was no real competitor for Mr Clements, having only four cows and retailing to late night customers. Edward sang harvest hymns as his bucket clanked from door to door and dipped the milk from his North Devon cows with a pint measure pouring it into the waiting jugs at cottage doors. Lavender grazed her way down the road just keeping up with her master.

'We plough the fields and scatter, All is safely gathered in', was a rural epilogue to the village as the bells rang and dogs whined and barked from their barrels.

Archie Butler the blacksmith cricketer from the Forest of Dean shod some of the horses in the village; but we had most of the repairs to our implements, and our horses shod, by someone whom Ralph called 'young Tom Higgins of Sedgeberrow'. Tom was a broad-shouldered man of about sixty. He had an eternal grin, wore damson-coloured corduroy trousers under his leather blacksmith apron. He specialized in repairing mowing machines and reaping machines; with scowl of brow he straightened the twisted bedding which held the fingers of these machines and rebuilt the painted work of Bamford or Bamlett and Massey Harris, canary yellow and vermilion red. His anvil stood by a long-handled guillotine, which cut cold metal. Under a black cobwebbed roof the brick chimney from his forge puffed smoke from the bellow-fanned fire.

All around him on the floor were broken pieces of farm implements waiting to be cured by his hammer. Broken driving bars from mowers which he shut-welded, making the two ends white hot in the fire, then fusing them together. He rasped the rough joint smooth in his vice. The multitude of nails on the walls held half-finished horse shoes ready to be fitted to Shires, nags and ponies by Bill Slatter the farrier.

Bill was a quiet, tall chap with black curly hair. He'd been a farrier in the army. Slatters were as thick on the ground in Gloucestershire as Bomfords in Worcestershire. As I pumped the cow horn on the end of the handles of his bellows, he turned the horse shoes in the fire with a pair of tongs, tongs made on his anvil. He'd take the half-made shoe out of the fire and hold it with the tongs on the rounded end of the anvil and beat it with his hammer. Back into the fire until the shoe was a near fit for Blackbird or Flower. Laying the shoe on the anvil white hot, he took a punch and made the holes to take the horse shoe nails. The punch went through like a hot knife in butter. Then over a hole in the anvil Bill finished the nail holes in the shoe.

Blackbird was tied in the stable alongside. Bill carried the shoe and lifted the horse's foot and put it between his leather aproned knees and fitted it hot on the hoof. The smell of burnt hoof as the metal bedded itself into the hard horn foot gave an unforgettable smell. When he took the shoe back to the anvil to make a minor adjustment, the bottom of Blackbird's hoof was left with a semi-circle of black, a pattern to receive the shoe.

After Bill had nailed the shoe on the hoof, he put Blackbird's foot on an iron stand and clenched the nails over on the top of the hoof then rasped away the outside until the shoe and hoof were tidy. When the shoeing was over, Bill allowed me to use a brush and paint the hooves with a black coloured oil. So the white and pink of Blackbird's feet were black for a while.

At his smithy I, like all boys, was also intrigued to see Bill Slatter make shut links. They were to mend broken plough traces made like a paperclip in quarter-inch round iron, threaded from one link to another then closed with a hammer, like putting a key on a keyring. Ralph the carter always carried shut links in his frail basket in case a snatching horse broke the traces.

Tommy The Journal on Fridays came to the bay window, puffing scented Woodbine smoke as he delivered the weekly paper. *The Journal* was twopence [1p] and sometimes Dad would leave it a couple of weeks before paying Tommy. 'How much do I owe you, Tommy?' Dad said after about three weeks. 'Just a shilling tonight, sir,' the reply came. Dad paid, but paid him weekly after that.

The Echo, delivered every night for a penny, gave us the news, local and national. I read the murder cases: Brown and Kennedy; Thorn who buried his wife in the fowl pen; Alfred Arthur Rouse who set fire to his car with a tramp inside and collected his life insurance; hangings, recounted with these last words: 'Thorn walked bravely to the scaffold.' I imagined the scene on those eight o'clock execution mornings; woke sometimes at night, and pictured the condemned cell where I gathered the man could have what he wanted for breakfast.

Tom Higgins the blacksmith never sent a bill, but we were entertained every six months when his motor bike and side car parked outside our house, bringing him and his black invoice book with a black piece of knicker elastic round it.

'Well, Tom, I've brought your bill,' he said to Dad. They were both named Tom.

'You haven't beared down too much on your pen, I hope,' Dad replied.

Tom Higgins grinned and took the elastic band from his book and passed it to Dad. 'Seven pounds fifteen shillings.'

'You can do better than that, Tom.' Dad took his cheque book and poised with his pen over the amount. 'Make it seven pound, Tom.'

'No, I can't do that, Bill's wages are gone up and the price of nails, everything.'

'Come on, Tom, it's easier to reckon seven pounds.'

This chat would go on for half an hour, each man talking of hard times until Tom Higgins said, 'Seven pound ten shillings then, Tom.' The cheque was made for that amount and I wondered whether the blacksmith had put on that extra five shillings, knowing that there would be the usual wheeling and dealing on both sides. 'A cup of cocoa and bread and cheese, Mr Higgins?'

'Thank you, Mrs Archer. I mustn't stay long, I've two more calls to make in the village.'

He did stay and tried to persuade me to join his club, The Cirencester and Tewkesbury Sick and Dividend Society. He was Chairman and sat in the corrugated iron village hall at their meetings with what he called, 'the big five'. They doled out the money for folks who were ill, had those on the carpet who stayed out after six o'clock at night when they were sick and stopped one week's sick pay.

An extra few shillings a week on top of the Panel money was a great help to the working man, but he was only allowed to own one share for in those days a man on the Panel couldn't draw more money than he did when at work. Self employed were treated differently, they could invest more, pay more a week and draw more when they were ill.

You may wonder why Tom Higgins drank cocoa and not cider. Back in 1900 Dad had persuaded the then young Tom to sign the Pledge. His father had been a heavy drinker, sometimes drunk at 6.30 in the morning. All his life Tom Higgins kept his Pledge, never touching a spot of strong drink.

CRICKET

There is nothing which brings the village folk together – rich and poor, gentry, labourers, boys and girls – like a village cricket match, especially if it's a needle match between two neighbouring villages. A Saturday in summer started with Fred Tandy the groundsman mowing the field with a horse-drawn gang-type mowing machine pulled by Tommy, Mr Bernard Nicklen's nag. Fred sat on a seat, steering the horse round the outfield. Tommy wore special leather boots over his iron-shod hooves to prevent his feet making marks on the almost sacred ground. Fred then mowed the wicket with a hand mower and with whitewash marked out the twenty-two-yard pitch. The outfield was so well cared for it would have been possible to make a wicket anywhere on the three-acre field known as 'The Naits'. Here the best village ground in the Vale attracted teams from the Worcester League including county players. No plantains grew among that golf-green-like turf, where a village wag made a jingle: 'Fred Tandy, very handy, He caught a mole in every hole, I hope the moles don't catch Fred Tandy.'

A gleaming white pavilion, the gift of Sir James Curtis, had two dressing rooms market HOME TEAM and VISITORS behind a veranda reserved for MEMBERS ONLY. The tea-room with trestle tables was at the rear. A yellow-and-blue flag was hoisted to the top of a white pole when cricket was played (the village colours). At one end, fenced with corrugated iron sheeting, was LADIES and GENTLEMAN while at the other end under a drooping red withy tree Fred Tandy boiled the water for the tea in a copper furnace, a furnace fuelled by wood and coal.

The scoring hut was under the hedge alongside the railway line. Here Mr Hugh Clements kept his score book while outside little boys hung the square tin numbers clocking up the score and the number of wickets fallen and what score the last man made. No one likes to be out for a duck, but our village folk liked to rub it in. When the last man made a duck, we didn't put a nought or 'O' on the score board, but our captain, a witty farmer, had a black tin number plate with a white duck like an Aylesbury, to show the ring of spectators how a batsman had fallen to score. Most visiting teams thought it quite funny but one rather splendid team with creased flannels and blazers took a dim view of this village exposure of one of their star batsmen who failed to score.

The gala day of village cricket was Whit Monday when an all-day match with Alcester and Ragley Park included a free salad lunch for all who came, this lunch provided by Sir James Curtis. The members and the two teams had their lunch in the pavilion while we boys ate ours on the boundary wooden benches on the grass.

The match I liked was with Dumbleton, they were a strong side and they had a good ground on the estate. The visitors arrived about 2.30 and changed into their gear. Our team was strengthened by Ewart Morrison who had a day off from playing for his county of Gloucestershire and had just been awarded his County Cap. Dumbleton batted first. Ewart bowled his fast deliveries from the pavilion end, while another pace bowler, Ern Farley, attacked from the other. Charlie Griffin, Dumbleton's opening bat, was in devastating form. Ern appealed to Charlie Moore, the hurdle-maker umpire, for an LBW decision against him, only to get the reply from Charlie, 'Not out, but if it occurs again it will be.'

The runs came thick and fast, for where the pitch was the boundary towards the main road the ground was bone hard. Charlie Griffin piled on the score as Ewart took wickets of numbers three, four and five. By nearly tea-time Dumbleton were 220 for 9 and Charlie Griffin had made 110. Ewart bowled a particularly fast ball which Charlie countered with bat and pad. 'LBW out,' Charlie the umpire called for us all to hear.

'He can't be out, Charlie, he played the ball with his bat.' Charlie thought a few seconds then replied, 'The ball hit him on the leg and any road I'm ready for my tea.'

After tea our opening batsmen went in and Ewart batted first wicket down as number three. A ball well wide of the leg stump, he padded away in true county fashion. 'Out,' Charlie cried after a half-hearted appeal from a slip fielder. Ewart walked to the pavilion with his County Cap, his nicely creased cream flannels, his county blazer. He passed the members sitting on the veranda, Sir James Curtis and Mr J. C. Nicklen puffing at their cigars, Dad and Mr Field in their Panama hats. I sat on the grass outside with Tom Whittle our cowman, who said to me, 'Ewart has just used a word about the umpire's decision as 'unt in the Bible or the Prayer Book.' The Aylesbury duck hung on a nail outside the scoring hut, our best batsman gone.

Wickets fell until Archie Butler the blacksmith took to the field at number six. He carried his bat on his shoulder like a sledgehammer. No cream flannels for Archie. Silver grey trousers from Evesham Bon Marché and a flat pancake cap. He wore a leather belt and broad braces over his shirt. He flailed at everything, knocking fours and sixes. The better the ball the harder he hit it. If the ball was pitched on the off stump he swung it to the square leg boundary – sledgehammer blows from this giant of the Forest of Dean, a dark swarthy man with a curl of black hair under the peak of his cap, his rolled-up sleeves showing arms like legs of mutton, brown and tattooed.

As the pick-up goods train steamed slowly through the station past the cricket field Archie with an almighty swipe hit the ball for six into an open goods waggon which went twenty miles to Gloucester. No one else had hit a ball to Gloucester before. Charlie Moore the umpire raised his hands above his head and signalled six to Mr Clements in the scoring hut. Soon after Archie was caught out on the boundary after scoring seventy. In the pavilion he swore he'd never stay out there and make seventy again because when he returned to the home team's dressing room the other players had drunk all the cider. The other wickets fell to the Dumbleton bowlers and we lost by about one hundred runs.

BEHIND CLOSED DOORS

Long before holidays with pay and even before the Saturday half holiday became the normal thing on the land, men worked Saturday afternoons and got paid at four o'clock, just in time to walk or go by train to town to get extras for the home. But, though there wasn't much free time, entertainment in winter did happen periodically. Farmers, despite bad times, hunted on Saturdays and played cards at night. They had a rota of visits where under some farmhouse inglenook their pencil-marked churchwarden clay pipes were handed around in a basket with the tobacco tin by the host. (Each man kept a pipe at the farmhouses.)

By the 'twenties, the working man had gained his half day on Saturday to work his garden or allotment. Evening entertainment was at the Recreation Room, an old army hut from the First World War. Sir James Curtis had provided a full-sized billiard table which cost him over a hundred pounds. A dry working men's club was formed, young men played quoits, dominoes, cards and billiards in the warmth of that long narrow wooden building, warmed by an anthracite stove and looked after by a custodian, Mr Parminter. He trimmed the chain-swinging oil lamps, ironed the billiard table, swept the floor, held the keys and kept order.

I call it a 'dry' club, for the committee decided that no drink was ever to be had there. Wedding receptions were held at the school if strong drink was on the menu. Whist drives were held there weekly but never in Lent, whist being one of the things to give up during the forty days. Village folk took their whist very seriously. They glowered at their partners when the wrong card was played on the green baize table. A man, who will be nameless, kicked the table over when he was losing at whist, but Mr Parminter usually kept strict discipline.

He was an amateur boxer, who taught the village lads the noble art. He was an ex-navy man who did everything to keep a community of young folk entertained for a few shillings a week. At whist drives some players took bottles of Rowland's beer and hid them under the raised floor where the wooden building stood on little brick piers. They swigged the beer outside the room at the interval or on their way to the corrugated enclosure, the urinal. The room even had a WC when there had been enough rain for the rainwater off the roof to fill a lead tank on stilts outside. When the room was taken down years later, a stack of empty Rowland Brewer (which closed in the 'thirties) beer bottles lay under the floor – collector's items.

Concerts at the Recreation Room were packed with village folk: one hundred and twenty sat on the hard yellow chairs and the forms alongside the walls. The heat from Mr Parminter's red hot stove sometimes became intense. Some nights the smell of drying clothes, sweat, dubbined boots, twist tobacco and heat was overwhelming compared with the frosty outside air: a place for 'flu germs, measles and every winter-borne complaint which fell like a plague after Christmas.

But the concerts were a respite for the farming folk; Ewart Morrison compèred these evenings. He had a good baritone voice. William Tyler's rendering of 'Trumpeter, What Are You Sounding Now?' brought the occasional tear. Then he recited, 'There's a Green Eyed Yellow Idol.' A lady from a neighbouring village sang. 'A fat little fellow with his Mammy's eyes' – all very moving stuff. Then Mr Charles Nicklen told us some very funny stories, making us all laugh and giving Shepherd Tidmarsh a bout of coughing. 'Yers a fisherman's friend, Alf,' his wife would say in a stage whisper.

The vicar sang, 'Tomorrow will be Friday, and we've caught no fish today.' John Ellis Bass, painter and decorator, brought a wad of music to put on top of the piano, his repertoire was endless. The concerts ended with 'The King'. Mr Parminter put out the lights and little candle lanterns created a torchlight procession homewards up the village street.

The event we all looked forward to was the Armistice tea when the ex-servicemen, wearing their medals, lined a couple of trestle tables to be treated to a beef and ham tea followed by masses of jelly and blancmange. All day long a team of women prepared the food and little Reggie Nind, a ginger bearded retired farmer known as Monkey Brand carried water from a stand pipe in our yard to the copper boiler. There was no water at the room. The business part, when someone was appointed to tend the flower garden at the back of the war memorial, followed the tea. The memorial was a cross with the words lettered on the Portland stone: 'These men were a wall unto us by night and day,' followed by the names of the seven or eight soldiers who were killed in the war. The gentleman who had planted and cared for the flowers was complimented by the chairman.

After the hand clapping had died down one man got to his feet with these words, 'Now the flowers I agree looked nice, but I've one complaint. In the army the big men stand at the back and the little men in front. Now last year Master S. planted big flowers in front and the little flowers at the back, poor little fellas peeping over the tall ones.'

Mr S. rose to his feet. 'I propose Mr C. tends the garden next year, I resign.' An electric moment of village politics.

The piano had been trundled down the village in the morning from the school on a sack truck by the station porter. It was out of tune but Ruth the pianist who was an accomplished musician on piano, organ and accordian, did her best when a yellow or black ivory didn't respond. Mr S. didn't trust the piano, he brought his tuning fork and sang tenor unaccompanied, 'The Campbells Are Coming, a ho ana a ho,' and 'The March of the Cameron Men'. Mr Charlie Nicklen told his stories. Hugh Clements sang 'The Hawthorn Tree', then a witty little piece:

Tom Jones he had a party on Tuesday of last week,
Joe Biggs was there as usual with all his sauce and cheek.
He said, 'You chaps, I just have pinched
A sovereign from a pal.
Shall we have smokes and drinks with it?'
I said, 'Of course we shall.'
We had brandies round and ninepenny smokes,
We quite enjoyed the spree.
We laughed, we roared, and chuckled aloud with glee.
We screamed, we howled, we thought the joke was fine,
I didn't know till afterwards, the quid was mine.

Mr Cotton was an expert with beef bones (preferably rib bones), which were played by holding two bones in each hand and clapping them together to accompany music and song. He recited:

I comes up from the country, but I beunt so very green,
I know that two and two be four,
And twice four 'unt eighteen.
I read a lot of things in books
And learnt a lot at school.
Folks trys to do me, but I does they,
Because I looks a fool.

The village thatcher, a man of over six feet who soldiered in the Balkans, stood beside that trestle table where the men of medals and ribbons sat beside him. Placing his thumb in his broad leather belt he sang, 'If those lips could only speak, those eyes could only see, from the beautiful picture in the golden frame.' Then there were tears from widows of men who fell in the war. Shepherd Tidmarsh, grey whiskered, weather beaten in his Sunday suit, always sang the same song:

THE FOX AND THE HARE

King Christians all on you I call,
If to pity you feel inclined,
Your care to bestow on a fellow full of woe,
For he's almost out of his mind.
For wives I've wed who are all gone dead,
My love it was labour in vain.
I've married and I've buried until I'm almost worried
And I'm sick with wives on the brain.

Chorus

The fox and the hare, the badger and the bear,
And the birds in the green wood tree,
And the pretty little rabbits all engaged in their habits,
They all have a mate but me.
The first on the stage was little Sally Sage,
She once was a lady's maid.
But she ran away on a very dark day,
With a fellow in the fried fish trade.
The next was a cook, for a beauty she was took,
I'll tell you the reason why,
Her leg it was a stump, on her back she had a hump,
And she had an awful squint in her eye.

Chorus

Another one to charm, was a girl from a farm,
Well skilled in the harrows and the plough.
She guarded the rigs of a lot of little pigs,
And she squeezed new milk from the cow.

She was sixteen stone, all muscle and bone,
And she looked with an awful leer.
She would have been mine, but she fell in a decline
Through swallowing a mouse in her beer.

Chorus

It was much the same when another one came,
With a purse as long as your arm,
All full of yellow gold, such a sight to behold,
With the heart of a miser warm.
Her only sin was her love for gin,
But it brought all our hopes to wreck,
For she slipped with her heel on a little orange peel,
And she tumbled down and broke her blessed neck.

Chorus

I could add to the score fully half a dozen more,
For my list goes a long way round.
One went o'er the sea for a better chap than me,
But the last I had through drink went mad,
In vain I tried to stop her,
For sad to my dismay, I discovered that one day,
She was slowly boiled to death in the copper.

Chorus

A SIGHT OF THE BULL

At the Old Manor Farm a stone wall surrounded a big cattle yard. The top end of the yard was sheltered by a long eighteenth-century cattle shed, an open shed with wooden pillars mounted on stone foundations to support the front of the building. Along the right hand side were four stalls with mangers, and stone troughs with running water off Bredon Hill. A hay or fodder store completed the buildings.

Joker our Hereford bull was chained to his manger in the bottom stall, the stone sett floor always ankle deep in straw litter, the door at the back securely bolted.

Joker's chain with the wooden block called a 'chog' interested me. He wore his chain all the time except when he was loose in the yard. The steel links shone like silver as the grease from his neck prevented rust while the rubbing of his head when feeding or just bored caused the chain to move up and down in the stapled ring and polish the metal even more. The chain was so different from the cows' chains for they only wore them an hour or so a day while the calves butted their udders and extracted the last drop of milk from their teats. Cows' chains were rusty, the bull's chain was a polished silver.

Joker was the pure bred Hereford son of Grannie, the cow that reared me. His name fitted him for, before the leather washer was fitted to the tee piece which went through the ring, he used to escape. He roamed the village at night and one night dropped his nose ring over an arrow headed garden rail and bawled loudly outside a widow's window until dawn.

I'd often wondered why this near ton weight of beef stood, day

Eager to serve

151

in, day out in a stall, fed on the best of the hay and cake and mangolds. To me he didn't contribute anything. Was it prestige to keep a bull to show visitors how handsome a Hereford was? My friend Frank and I guessed that Joker had some connection with the cows calving every year although Dad had told me that he kept a bull because by doing so the cows gave more milk.

Frank and I were whipping our tops by the village green. We liked the tall fliers and with a whip of pudding string on a nut stick we made them fly. A sound of a cow bawling came from near the Post Office. In fact there were two cows, both Shorthorns, a red one and a roan. Every so often the red one rode piggyback on the roan. Frank smiled, looked at me and said, ''Tis Master Baldwyn and Blenheim bringing the cows to our bull.'

I watched a minute and saw the upright Mr Baldwyn, breeched and gaitered, carrying a cane walking stick. Struggling to keep up with master and the cows, Blenheim propelled his arthritic frame by a long ash plant. The cows stopped under a lilac tree, the roan stood as firm as a rock while the red one mounted. Blenheim had caught up and swung his ash plant and called, 'Come on now, we 'un't stopping yer.'

Frank and I nipped through the churchyard down by Tythe Court and hid ourselves among the beans in a stall next to the bull. Tom our cowman met the men at the double gates and turned the cows into the yard. He then untied the bull. Frank and I lay as quiet as mice and watched the bull charge around the strawed yard until he came near the roan cow. His nostrils sniffed the air, they opened and shut like two mouse traps. His nose rivelled, his eyes glazed. He pawed the straw, then stood alongside the roan who cocked her tail then put her tail on one side and mounted the bull. When this happened Frank and I noticed a discharge like frog spawn come from under her tail and stick as saliva to her tail. Joker made a pass at the roan, from a sheath under his belly his long tool emerged red and raw looking. It leaked a little and dripped against the roan cow's flanks. Joker took a sniff under her tail; this excited him. His nostrils rivelled and what we called his prick emerged further from the hiding place of its sheath. Then suddenly Joker mounted the cow and like an arrow shot his prick, pierced the cow under her tail and disappeared as if flattened by the exertion. Joker slipped off the roan's back.

The cow's tail stood erect and as the bull penetrated her body she put her tongue out between her lips. Both animals stood there one behind the other and Blenheim laughed and shouted, 'Let her have another go for luck.'

Joker pawed the ground then sniffed the roan until his nostrils and his sheath altered shape and once more he entered the cow's passage on the only day that month it would be possible.

The red cow stood uninterested, she was not willing to be coupled with Joker on that day. Tom the cowman wrote a record in his book that Mr Baldwyn's roan had been served and he collected the seven shillings and sixpence [37½p] off the farmer. Frank and I slid off the beams a bit too soon, for Blenheim saw us and threatened to what he called, 'Acquaint thee Fayther.'

We had seen something that day which one day would be commonplace to me. Just a cow and a bull doing what came naturally, but it was so sudden. It's true there were overtures before the actual coupling, but the act of union was swift, short lived. Two things amazed me, the length of the bull's penis when it emerged from its sheath and the size of his testicles. No one had told us anything, but we just guessed that all creatures had this in common, that the male fertilized the female. The cockerel on the muck heap with the hens, the drake on the pond with the ducks, and Shepherd Tidmarsh's Suffolk rams with raddled breasts who left their marks on the backs of the Kerry ewes they served in October.

Could it be that we came that way? We heard stories at school, while every spring was called 'mackintosh time' on Bredon Hill for couples, who, regardless of the sun, walked arm in arm through the churchyard carrying a mackintosh. Frank and I watched some cuddling and canoodling under the Paris Hill oaks, but we kept far enough away not to be seen. Then in a hayfield on a hot July Sunday afternoon we imagined we saw a couple do very much the same as Joker had with the roan. It seemed obvious that the population of man and beast was continued in the same fashion.

Girls to us seemed silly, giggly, and so unlike their mothers, and we had no idea how to talk to them. Cricket on the footpath was exclusively for boys while at parties we met the girls and felt them to be different, but never admitted kissing one. That would be sissy for a boy of eleven.

THE MAC-CARRYING SEASON

Every year about Eastertime on Sunday afternoons when the
spring sunshine glistened the snow-white blackthorn, Frank and
I used to see young couples walk arm in arm past the drooping ash
trees in St Barbara's churchyard. The mac-carrying season had
arrived. No matter how fine the day, the young girls' escort
carried a mackintosh. We wondered why. 'Let's follow 'um,' we
both said together.

A favourite haunt of the couples who did what was known as
sweethearting was beneath the Cuckoo Pen, a clump of beeches
on Little Hill. Here a rocky escarpment had created a ledge like a
seat, a little platform of stone. From the gorse bushes near Paris
Hill hedge I saw the overtures of love for the first time.

We were only twelve years old – a state of flux between boy and
man. The somewhat clumsy caresses of a country chap and his
maid sparked off a deep emotion in me which I didn't understand. Why did a chap in his teens get together with a girl just
starting in domestic service?

'He's got her on his knee,' Frank whispered.

'I'll go to Hanover,' I replied.

They kissed and cuddled for a while then the mackintosh was
laid down sort of reverently on the wild-thyme-scented turf of
the hill. They lay side by side, quite still, then he put daisies in her
plaited hair and stroked her heaving breasts. Enfolded in each
others arms with their lips together, the sweethearts lay and I
wondered what it all meant. Would I ever feel that way? Was this
the inexplicable thing between lovers? Where would it lead?
Surely not to what Frank and I had seen when the bull coupled
with a cow in season. That would be awful.

Going home to tea, the sweethearts left behind on the hill, we
decided that next Sunday afternoon, like stalkers of deer, we'd be
camouflaged in the gorse and learn just how the overtures of love
had happened on the hill since time began.

We took a cheap return on the train to Evesham on a Saturday
night where, at the Scala Cinema, Frederick March starred in 'We
Live Again'. The love scenes in the conservatory just made me
wonder if this was real life, was it how a fellow should be with a
beautiful woman.

At the Mop Fair, after spending a few coppers on the swing

boats, the coconut shies, I saw a sequined half-dressed woman seducing men into a tent where she promised to show the packed onlookers everything. 'Everything,' I said to Frank. On a little stage, lit with gas lamps, we stood in semi-darkness, open mouthed at the disrobing of this female. When only a little belt of fur covered her crutch, she danced and did cartwheels on the platform of wood. The music played, she came down among her patrons and with bared breasts brushed me. 'What did you think?' I asked Frank on the homebound train.

'Dunno,' he replied. 'I don't like women very much, I'll never get married.'

I replied, 'She made me feel ever so strange inside.' We never discussed it again; the couples of the hill were more real, I thought they were fond of each other.

Frank and I smoked Sarony cigarettes on the hill when sixpence [2½p] could be found for a packet of ten, maybe in defiance of what some said at Chapel, that if we smoked down here we would smoke in hell. When we had no cigarettes for Sunday afternoons to give a balm between morning and night at Chapel, there was a rick of clover by Great Hill barn. Here I did what generations before had done – rubbed the clover blows. How I like that word of Shakespeare's for blossom. The blows made a tolerable smoking mixture and a penny clay pipe burnt the fuel.

Sometimes little groups of village girls passed as, sitting under a wall, the bonfire-like smoke wafted in blue eddies from the clays. They giggled and walked by holding their heads up high. I quite fancied one with golden curly hair but just took a deep breath and Frank said, 'We haven't clicked,' 'clicking' being a word used when a boy and girl noticed something inexplicable in each other which drew them close together.

One Sunday afternoon we cycled to Dumbleton, meeting a couple of girls near the little hamlet of Didcot. Two sisters, I remember; one's name was Mary. We were much too green for them. They just laughed at us so the next week the clover rick and the clay pipes under the wall passed the time of day and mac-carrying to the Cuckoo Pen seemed ages away and I decided I'd never be seen carrying a mac up St Barbara's churchyard.

Frank cycled alone to Tewkesbury the following week, meeting a girl on the Mythe bridge. He told me she was too

clinging, coming from Spring Gardens. He left her in the twilight
but came home a little more educated in the art of sweethearting;
he decided not to meet her again.

I had walked along by the Cuckoo Pen that Sunday and met
Celia up there. No Mary Pickford or Olivia de Haviland, but just
a girl of thirteen summers. That hot summer's day she wore a
flowered crêpe de chine dress and soon we were holding each
other close together by the Parker's Hill hedge. I kissed her and
the first bite of the apple put my head into a Catherine wheel
which span round until only a spark remained of the flame. 'After
Chapel, on Didcot Ham by Carrants Brook, we'll meet, shall
we?' She nodded. We went home to tea our separate ways.

I took little notice of the sermon that evening and if the
preacher described the lake of hell fire it passed over my head
melting like butter in the sun.

It was about 7.30 when Celia met me down Gypsies Lane by
Didcot Ham gate. What a disappointment, for Celia, coming
straight from the church choir, wore a navy blue, what was
known as a costume, and some sort of hat to match. Holding her
under the leaning withy trees was like holding just one of those
trees, a whalebone corsetted body unresponsive to any caress.
She felt like a chainmailed soldier. The soft feminine bosomy
experience of the Sunday afternoon had been covered in top
security.

'Why did you change, Celia?' I said haltingly.

'The choir of course, I'm in the choir.'

I thought, damn the Church and Chapel if that's what it does,
camouflaging the sparkle of youth and putting a barrier between
two young bodies.

That night in bed I had a wet dream, a beautiful yet frightening
experience and next day a lecture, a kind lecture from Dad
explaining the danger of such an experience: danger to health,
danger that the change into full manhood would be stunted.

Monday at school was a daylight dream. Just going through
the motions of lessons, like Sunday at Chapel, the teaching had as
much chance of being memorized in my brain as a snowball in
hell.

After tea and a minimum of homework, I walked the dog to
Paris Gardens, meeting a football friend, Albert. 'You were out
with Celia last night,' he said angrily.

'Yes, why?' I replied.

'Do that again and I'll give you a bloody hiding.' Celia was apparently Albert's girlfriend. In a way I was glad: she was not worth fighting for.

Life with Frank on the hill on hot Sunday afternoons was like being on an island; no more than a mile from the village, yet a place where we planned the sort of chaps we would like to be and the kind of life we would like to live.

The mac-carrying couples were thinner on the ground by September and by autumn and winter the caressing and canoodling would be confined to the tallets, the hay lofts above the stable.

It was one September Sunday afternoon when Frank and I walked along Carrants Brookside. A late crop of hay was still in cocks ready for carrying. The rain had stained the fodder to a battle ship grey colour. The cocks had been there maybe three weeks. 'Look,' Frank called out. As he called, a quist or wood pigeon's wings made the ivy leaves which covered the pollard withy like giant hats flutter whirlwind-like. 'A late nest,' I said.

'No,' Frank replied, 'yonder, Amy and Norman doing their courting.'

We stood behind a withy afraid we would be seen. I nodded to Frank towards a split withy tree which had conveniently fallen across the brook making a perfect bridge to cross. We crossed, then climbed another tree and sat among the ivy. Water voles peeped from the banks, moorhens splashed as they swam with their half grown chicks to and fro. It was so peaceful, peaceful as September should be after the August storms.

'Yonder,' Frank whispered. Norman chased Amy around the hay cocks. They sparred like March hares; he held her and kissed her. Then his strong arms carried her like a doll, dropping her on top of a cock of hay. She threw handfuls of hay at him, and punched his broad shirt fronted chest. A loving punch.

In March I had watched the hares on the hill for hours doing their mad mating, Jack hares boxing like men, somersaulting like clowns, then for no apparent reason running away in a dead straight line out of sight for a while until the whole comedy started all over again. Hares would gather in groups quite unconscious of my ringside seat. I'd been so close to them, closer than Frank and I would venture towards Norman and Amy. In a lesser

157

degree the ram made similar overtures to his mate before the symphony of coupling and leaving his telltale red mark of raddle on the ewe's rump.

Norman chased Amy towards our tree. She fell in his arms on a cock of hay quite close to the brook. 'Quiet,' Frank whispered, 'he's pulling her knickers down.' I sighed, trembled a little as his hands slid up under her dress like a doctor examining a patient. He pulled her dress gently over her head, then her petticoat.

'He's holding her tits,' I whispered to Frank.

'Shush, shush,' Frank whispered back.

They lay quite still for a while, Amy's hands clasped around Norman's neck. Unbuttoning his trousers he inserted his stiff, pink candle-like organ between her wide open legs. She winced. Norman agitated his movements as regular as the piston on our oil engine, until at last Amy called as if in an agony of delight, 'Norman, Norman.'

It was all over. They lay there as still as death, then the young couple brushed the hay from each other's clothes. Norman gently pulled the black knickers over Amy's feet to their rightful place. As smart as paint they walked away arm in arm towards the Ham and the roadway. Frank and I climbed from our tree, agreeing that we had experienced something never seen by us before on the hill. Something rather frightening at thirteen years old. Yet parts were so beautiful and Norman was gentle for a farm labourer of nineteen who was used to the horses and cows.

'Perhaps he loves her,' Frank said.

'Dunno,' I replied. We went home to tea.

The following year at Easter a couple who had made their promises in each other's arms near the Cuckoo Pen decided to marry: Bob who worked on a market garden and Clara a young dressmaker. The usual throng around the old village cross watched Bob and his best man in navy suit walk under the drooping ashes to St Barbara's Church to await his bride. A simple affair; no cars, but pretty dresses and flowers and well-wishers, with a little reception at the bride's cottage up the lane.

Bob was a bell-ringer, so the five bells spoke messages of good will loud and clear. In those days in the 'twenties, the little cliché 'unknown destination' was not the local press's way of keeping folks guessing where the bridal couple had gone for their honeymoon. It was Weston-super-Mare. Where else did the train go for about six shillings [30p] return?

Frank and I didn't like weddings. For me everything seemed so feminine, a bit childish in a way with confetti and rice. The photographs were the worst. I hadn't forgotten spending a hot afternoon outside a marquee while a black-hooded photographer tried again and again to get his pictures. It was my cousin's wedding, but the bridegroom took umbrage and refused to be photographed. It took strong men strong words to get this young man into a picture. Maybe he regretted tying the knot with a gold ring that morning.

Bob and Clara after the reception walked arm in arm past our house for the railway station. No fuss, no car, no silly games. Bob was a sensible chap and Clara a tall, rather prudish young lady. They were both middle aged in my eyes, thirty years old.

The following Saturday, Ralph, Harry, Charlie, Tom and Len walked up the churchyard about a quarter to seven in the evening. I wondered why they were going to ring. One, two, three, four, five, they chimed. The bells were ringing a welcome home to the bride and her groom. The little tank engine pulled in a couple of coaches at seven o'clock, hissing steam, belching smoke from its funnel, then, as Mr Marshall the guard blew his whistle, it puffed away, a bit breathless up the incline to Stanborough Crossing. Bob and Clara crossed the level crossing, walked the railway yard to the Groaten Lane and heard the bells. What a way, I thought, to greet a fellow ringer.

I saw them smilingly turn the corner under our rickyard elms, the bells ringing no doubt in their ears. As if someone told the ringers just when the couple would pass the cross near the church, Charlie, captain of the tower, schooled his men to fire the bells so that all five rang like the guns of the 1812 overture. Magic

to me, a boy, to see the smiles on Bob and Clara's faces and hear the clapping from a little group of well wishers sitting on the cross. To me that was the wedding rather than the ritual of the previous Saturday.

BACKYARDS

The rustic larch porches of the village cottages were hung with clematis or rambler roses to blend with the black and white squares of the cottage walls. Front doors were often drably painted, an orangey brown, with heavy hinges. No one seemed interested in scraping the layers of lead paint away to expose the beauty of unstained oak. Only Mr Hughes, the artist's door was different. His was shining white and the door handle a knob of cut glass.

The little backyards of the cottages were a hive of industry, especially in summer. Here the firewood was cut and split. A door led to the privy, another to the wash house and a little below the pig sty and a shed. The accumulation of years of working on the land hung on great nails from the back walls of the cottage and in the shed; a long galvanized bath ready for its weekly Friday night exercise; a breast plough for use on the allotment; hoes, forks, jadders (stock axes), scratters (small harrows), spring balances, steelyards (weighing machines), a pig ladder, a pig bench, buckets, pot hooks, sickles, scythes – cobwebbed but ready for their particular season.

The wash house was an inferno of steam on Monday mornings as the copper boiler, laced with soap, soda and Reckitt's blue, made the sheets white again to exhibit to the neighbours on the long wire clothes line. The smell from the flue told tales of the cremation of pig bones, old shoes, worn-out shirts and trousers. All went under the boiler with slack coal, sprout stems and wood. The knack of creating such a fire which drew was something I never understood.

The fires indoors often had to be coaxed to burn well. Then the smoke would weep under the beam of the chimney breast. But these magic furnaces for washday roared like little lions and

SALLY.

consumed all the weekly waste which was unfit for the pig wash tub.

In those little courtyards a battery of orange boxes held the native caged birds. Approaching the back door the greetings of jackdaws and magpies welcomed me at the Hunting, Whittle or Cotton households. 'Morning, hello?' the jackdaw's little nasal, almost human, speech came from behind the lattice wire in front of the orange box. It didn't matter what time of day, it was always, 'Morning.' The magpie came to and fro from its box at will, sitting on my shoulder, looking for something to steal and fly away with. Being prepared for the reception, I'd give him a broken biscuit from my pocket and he would say, 'Thank you,' and fly to the top of the wash house and eat it and return.

There was something very special about those backyards; often approaching a house there can be a certain sterility of a porch, a tidy door step, a mat, maybe an upturned bucket, but all is dead, silent. But then the rural community embraced the creatures of the woodland and field, took them to their hearts as brothers and sisters of the world. The jackdaw, magpie or caged blackbird became members of the family. They entered and left their roosts at will. They all had a story: a fledgeling fallen from the nest and picked up and nurtured by a farmhand's wife to please her children, perhaps.

I often wondered why we kept rabbits when the hill was alive with them, but the Chinchilla, the Belgium hare and the Old English graced many of the courtyards. Fed on dandelions, grass, cabbage and oats and bran from the granary they grew and multiplied until when their numbers became so big and the boxes crowded, we took them on the hill and in the great earths or warrens they crossed with their ancestors of the wild so that a multi-coloured society integrated, black and white, sandy and grey.

Some cottages had large wire cages in the gardens where goldfinches sang, nested and bred. There was always something secretive about the goldfinch breeders. The thistle blows on the hill were a haven for these pretty songsters, but how the birds came to the wired corrals for breeding, for sale, for crossing with canaries to produce what was known as a Mule, was mysterious. Some said Jack Hunting caught them with bird lime – that illegal ticky tack once common in the country. The birds' feet got caught up in the bird lime traps set on wooden perches among the thistles. I never knew, but knew some cottagers who bred goldfinches for sale and often listened to their song by the back door of the houses.

It's odd how the rarities of childhood – the bullfinch in particular – have now became a plague to the fruit grower. I hardly ever saw a bullfinch as a boy except the one in a glass case on the piano. The seagull was only seen in times of very bad weather and as boys we'd say, 'I saw a seagull today.' Now they are commonplace.

'Did they split a jackdaw's tongue to enable him to talk?' I asked Jack the carpenter. Jack grinned and showed me his latest lot of ferrets, little balls of cream fur lying with the mother, the gill. In another box his big black-and-white Fitcher ferret, the hob, clawed at the wire for food as Jack gave it liver, bread and milk; the skunk-like smell still lingers in my memory.

Jack handled his furry creatures like a child with a new doll. They crawled up his bare arms into his pockets. He loved his ferrets. Then one day pandemonium reigned as Jack's big hob broke loose into a neighbour's fowl pen and slaughtered eight laying hens. A sorry sight when Jack returned to dinner to see the hens bitten in their necks and killed and the ferret asleep in the pen as full of blood as a blowed tick. That cost poor Jack four shillings [20p] for each hen but he plucked the birds and sold them at a few pence to neighbours for the pot. I wondered how the hob ferret escaped, for Jack was so particular with fences of all kind, his maxim being, 'Safe bound, safe found.'

ALBANY VALE

Before ever the term youth club was coined, the lads of the village when they became about thirteen years old met at Albany Vale's cottage. Albany had a son, a love child, Bill. He was all she had got and although he was about nineteen years old, he was a misfit, but the young lads liked to sit in the cottage winter nights and listen to his tales.

He taught them to use a button and stick it to somebody's

window by hanging a length of cotton to it and sticking the cotton to the glass with a bit of glue of some sort. The cotton reel was unwound to a hedge bottom some twenty yards away and the cotton pulled, then the button kept tapping on the window. He was an annoying sort of lad, and often I've seen PC Smith draw his walking stick across his shoulders.

Albany had two long front teeth. She was very bent and witchlike, yet kind to the boys in the village. She bought a gramophone with the legend 'His Master's Voice' and the picture of the little dog listening to the record. It had a horn speaker.

Albany's cottage had an open fire on the hearth, which Bill fed with great logs of wood, and a bread oven where Albany baked the bread. The boys sat around the fire, some with reddened faces, in the ingle while Bill put on the gramophone records. All the old tunes, but every time a new record came out the boys put their pennies together and bought it.

I saw them in the fire and candlelight, the rose-patterned wallpaper, the white scrubbed table where they played dominoes and the new invention, the gramophone. No wireless, just records, and the local paper that Bill collected from the station; hot news from Cheltenham – football, murders, weddings, the lot.

After Bill had organized the paper round, delivering to the few folk who could afford *The Cheltenham Echo*, roast potatoes cooked in the embers were for all who came. It was here that Bill shared his Woodbines. The boys shared theirs, and Albany made cups of cocoa. A very informal club.

Sometimes Bill would bring cider home from the farm where he worked and then the singing started. Singing with gramophone accompaniment. These were Albany's entertainers, Bill's friends.

Aunt Beatrice who lived next door hated her nephew because he ran up and down with the boys along a narrow passage between the two cottages. Bill always got the blame when the boys put thunderflash fireworks under Beatrice's door. She had been known to empty the chamber pot on them from the bedroom. Albany just grinned, put another log on the fire, some more potatoes in the embers.

Christmas at Albany's was great fun. The boys were too young to go to the Star Inn opposite. Bill fetched the cider, Albany warmed it over the fire lacing it with nutmeg, rosemary, then rationed it to the boys.

Sometimes PC Smith looked in at the unofficial club. He knew if the boys were in there they wouldn't be up to mischief. The club went on for many years. Boys came, left, and went to the pub or to play billiards at the Recreation Room where they were not allowed until they were sixteen.

Bill never married, and when Albany broke her hip and gave up the club, something very precious went from the village: a roof for boys to gather, a fireside with music they would remember. I remember.

A RING FENCE

One often hears the criticism that country folk are too parochial. Nowadays that may be a valid criticism, but what of the 'twenties? My feelings of parochialism gave me a sense of security as a boy; meeting the same old faces day after day, feeling safe from all that was happening in the big wide world was bliss. Being reared on a five hundred acre farm was to live in a small society for no one from outside came to direct the ways of the land.

'Thou hast put a fence around they servant Job,' I read in the Bible. The fence remained until Job's troubles, but with his cattle and his sheep he had been a kind of monarch in what he held dear. There were lots of little fences in our parish and a larger fence around it. Villages adjoining were foreign, and a gentle, simple rivalry pervaded between them. Even in the market town of Evesham, crossing the bridge over the Avon to Bengeworth, known as Donneybrook, was to go to a foreign land. One belonged one side or the other of that river.

Dad was not alone in the fear that maybe one day we should be ruled from Whitehall. It seemed dreadful. Certainly there was poverty but almost everyone was relatively poor, there were no great differences. And there were plenty of good things: I well remember eating my first foreign apple in June when apples were out of season. It seemed like the end of a way of self-sufficiency, almost a crime.

Everything was eaten fresh, in its season, including peas, until a factory was set up at nearby Ashchurch to can peas. Lincolns were the variety. The little factory bought from the growers and Dad and Mr Bailey his partner grew them free of mildew on Bredon Hill to pick in September for the factory. Another factory at Evesham canned peas. They called themselves Concentrated Limited.

It was a cold December Sunday when the usual sprouts, potatoes and meat for dinner were suddenly changed. Dad bought a tin of peas. The unnatural green look of them when they were tipped into a colander was too verdant for fresh peas. Dad looked at the emerald corn from the pea pod. He smelt it as the thick liquor dripped through the holes in the colander. 'Looks like vitriol to me,' he said as we dubiously sniffed the contents of the can. He swilled and rinsed them under the tap until the evil-looking liquid had all gone down the sink. Then they were cooked and that Sunday dinner was the first and last where peas were the second vegetable from a can.

I remember how as a boy with other boys I enjoyed in that ring fence around the five hundred acres of our farm a playground where no one told us to keep to the footpaths, where the only forbidden places sacrosanct were the sheep barn or the peeping spring onions along Beckfords Way. We could stray all over Bredon Hill on neighbours' land provided the rules were observed, rules such as keeping Rip the dog on a lead amid a neighbour's sheep and confining the use of our air guns and catapults to the five hundred acre ring.

Even the village road was metalled from stone dug from the parish quarry. Tarmac and the hard stone from the Clee Hill hauled from the station had come to the main road. But that was the county council's province while our road was maintained by the Pebworth Rural District Council and the Parish Council.

At the grammar school I had learned with interest of an eighteenth-century Scot named Macadam and how he invented a new way of road making. Watching the Macadam system applied in the village street was a slow process of many men, many horses and a steam roller from Bomford and Evershed of Salford Priors perfecting a tolerable surface with native materials.

First of all the large rocks of Bredon Hill limestone were rolled in. Backwards and forwards the driver pressed the foundation until it was level. The one armed driver on the roller with his leather-peaked cap left a haze of smoke and steam as he chuffed back and forth. He kept the engine in the cart track to Tythe Court overnight and for that privilege made a road there. The men with wheelbarrows wheeled the smaller stones from the heaps on the grass verge and tipped them onto the rebuilt road.

Then Mr Spires with his two lovely strawberry roan horses followed with loads of gravel and some soil. The water cart pulled by another of Mr Spires's team sprayed water over the mixture until the whole mass resembled a muddy pie; but the steam roller welded the lot together until the surface was a kind of concrete. Chuff, chuff, chuff, the great roller spoke as the road became an example of eighteenth-century engineering. A finish of gravel and sand gave a grey fawn top which settled in the summer sun, a highway for the horse traffic and the few cars. It's true the road became a bit muddy in winter, but Stodge Warren the roadman maintained it, filling the pot holes and with a stock axe did what was known as 'siding', a way of keeping the grass back from encroaching onto the road.

The impression was of slow patient work which compacted a mass of material from the hill and the sandpit into a good district council road. The slowness of the steam roller and the number of journeys it made was the essence of the operation. I gather little was done in new road-making from Roman times until Macadam's day in the late 1700s, and when the railways came, even that was restricted.

Fences of all kinds had been a special interest of mine since a very small boy.

'Who owns this fence?' I often asked Tom the stockman.

He would answer, 'You should know, Fred, that fence is owern, the ditch is on the t'other side to our field.'

The ditch was the boundary since Enclosure Acts of 1783 when ditches were dug to mark out the new fields and the soil thrown up on the owner's side. It was on these mounds that the hawthorn hedges were planted, hence dividing fences were known as mounds, while the repair of fences was called mounding. Both fence and ditch were the responsibility of the owner of the mound. Barbed wire was in little use when I was a boy, although invented during the Crimean War.

I watched Jack the rough carpenter mending gaps in the mounds with split withy poles and stakes. The brookside withy trees were religiously lopped every seven years and the poles stacked for fencing material. The green withy was easy to split with a cleaver by tapping this right-angled cutting tool into the heart of the pole at the small end. If the splitting was attempted at the butt end of the pole, the cleaver when twisted would leave the core or heart of the pole and come out maybe halfway in its track. 'Allus start at the little end of a pole and the big end of a woman,' was Jack's philosophy. I learnt that a split pole lasted longer than a round pole as a fencing rail especially if the bark was removed, for when it dried, it dried hard, and would bridge the gap for several years until the hawthorn grew and the gap in the hedge was secured.

The tallest wooden fence I saw as a boy was around Elmley deer park. The stakes were eight feet long and made of harder woods than withy for they were cleft oak and ash. Despite this fence the deer escaped in the late 'twenties and formed a little herd on the hill and in winter did some damage to the crops.

Jack the carpenter used to snare them in their well worn tracks through the bracken and elder with steel snares like badger snares. Jack being a mysterious character, no one ever knew exactly what he was about. He really ought to have been a gamekeeper, but confined himself to using what he called maxims: things like catching rabbits alive for the shooters with knots in his snares so that the rabbits could be retrieved alive.

The remains of a fence which had lasted hundreds of years between the Church and Chapel now had gaps, wide gaps like the deer fence in Elmley park. The remembrance of the old folk was vivid: tales of Archdeacon Timbrel, vicar from 1795 until 1865 were still being told. Timbrel was an autocrat, a Squarson, and had no time for the ranters of nonconformity. Likewise the Chapel folk viewed the established church as full of what was known as mumbo jumbo where the truth was veiled by psalm singing and crossing, bowing and scraping in front of the eagle.

The vicar in my day was Rev. W. W. Baker, a diplomat, a twentieth-century George Herbert. No, the ploughmen didn't stop their teams when the church bell rang for morning prayer, but Wilson Baker practised a name type of Christianity: he was a diplomat, a leader, a man to whom anyone could talk, and who always found some good thing to say of an old villager at his funeral. Wilson Baker quietly and inconspicuously welded a flimsy bond between the two churches. He had an ally in Mr Bernard Nicklen. It took a deal of courage to walk from the bottom of the village and the Church to the top and the Chapel, for this Church of England lay preacher to mount the rostrum at the chapel and give his experiences in the faith to a nonconformist congregation. But Bernard Nicklen did just that. He did it in chapels of the Bredon Hill area. Old habits die hard, and some of the staid devotees of the Establishment frowned on his catholic faith. The gap in the fence between the nonconformists and the Establishment was widened as some thinking people began to say that it was one God we worshipped.

This became more apparent to me at harvest festivals when on different Sundays the two churches were full of a lot of villagers of both persuasions. Not unity in all respects, but an understanding, a little village federation when confirmation and conversion were still the main facets of faith.

THE GENTRY, MIDDLE CLASS AND OTHERS

There was an accepted class distinction in village life; I thought of four classes being the strata of village life. At the top of the tree of power and respect was Mr John Baldwyn, the last of a family of squires who had been looked up to for six hundred years. He walked frock-coated to Church every Sunday morning and I always touched my cap to him. Apparently he was a quite accessible gentleman, but to me he was just a little lower than the King.

A little below him was Dr Roberson, who had married into the Baldwyn family and was Chairman of the Parish Council, the District Council, the School Board and the Guardians; he had the bearing of a country gentleman, with close-cropped beard, box hat, walking stick and his smart horse and trap. Beside that, he was often the mediator between life and death when farm labourers were ill. A father figure indeed.

When Mr J.C. Nicklen had come to the village and bought up several farms early in the century he took the place of the two previous gentlemen in lots of ways. As a landowner and employer of labour he made a mark in village life despite the fact that he still worked as an iron master in Smethwick and travelled to Birmingham regularly by train. Known affectionately as the Old Gentleman, he had a liveried chauffeur and two gardeners, and to my mind, he, and he alone, held the reins in village life.

Together with a friend of his, Sir James Curtis, knighted for his work as Food Minister for the Midlands during the Fourteen War, Mr J.C. Nicklen travelled First Class to Birmingham, a thing unique in the village. He smoked big cigars and cases of liquid refreshment were delivered by the station porter to his rather grand house known as The Close. I always felt afraid to speak to him while we waited for the 8.50 train.

George Hughes, an artist, lived with his wife at Orchard Cottage. He was a traveller on our train, an immaculate gentleman who had been to school with no less a person than Lord Birkenhead. That impressed me no end. George Hughes carried a little leather case. What was inside was a mystery. To me he was the kindest of the gentry to us boys, both as a friend and for his generosity.

Every day when the 4.05 train pulled into our little station, we looked for Mr Hughes. Was he on the train? If he was he took a number of pennies from his pocket for us to get a bar of Nestlé's chocolate from the slot machine. We gathered around him, then he slid a penny under our collars until it fell through our trouser legs onto the platform. A form of ritual which was enacted time and time again. He even invited us to his studio to look at his paintings, and when he came to our house for tea, there was always a sixpenny piece [2½p] for me. His soft velour trilby hat covered a mystery which I never knew until years after. His curly auburn hair had a circular kiss curl above his brow. I'm so glad I never knew it was a wig, for he was as bald as a coot.

It's debatable what a real gentleman really is, but my young mind sorted him out above the rest when I saw him raise his trilby hat to the woman who did his washing, salute the roadman Stodge Warren and hand him a shilling or an ounce of tobacco. George Hughes never went to church, but called himself a Free Thinker, whatever that meant.

It has been said that there are only three classes in the social scale. Those who are, those who wish they were, and those who don't care a damn whether they are or not. I saw four classes in the village: the gentry and those with money and position, including farmers; the middle class of blacksmiths, station masters, etc; the smallholders, self-employed and the leaders of workmen, like our shepherd; finally, casual and day labourers.

Bunch Baldwyn lived in one of our cottages near the church – a Florence Nightingale of the village in the 'twenties. Not a do-gooder, but a doer of good, for without her, life for the poorer folk would have been poorer still; Bunch was an amateur nurse. She was eccentric in the nicest way, but had a vision. 'For without a vision, the people perish.' It was not the little comforts of food, delicacies and drink that she purveyed to the ailing and the elderly, it was the fact that someone cared for them as their lives ebbed to their inevitable close.

I wondered sometimes how many gallons of beef tea, blackcurrant tea and bottles of wine and brandy she took with her to the elderly poor of the parish. How many raspberry blancmanges and jellies helped to ease the invalids and gave them a feeling that life was still worthwhile.

Mistakes she made, for she was an amateur nurse. Jack Hunting our rough carpenter was immobilized by lumbago. Daily Bunch massaged his painful back with embrocation while his doctor, in those far off days, gave him aspirin as the only pain killer. Bunch decided that a mustard poultice would possibly cure Jack's lumbago. The poultice prepared and, applied very hot, blistered his back; but soon Jack was around again, and forgave her.

She always played the organ at funerals. Bunch was an excellent organist and at funerals she really gave the farewell in an inimitable style. Playing the 'Dead March in Saul', Bunch made me feel that the music was not wholly of this earth, but a halfway house between earth and heaven. The organ blower knew from experience that Bunch would need all the wind that the bellows could pump through the pipes. He pumped away and I noticed the little brass indicator being kept right at the top of its track. It usually bobbed up and down like a fisherman's float, but not at funerals with Bunch at the organ. Knowing very little of church organs, but realizing that Bunch pulled out the stops and played her very best, the bass notes of this well-known finale to a departed one blasted the whole church. Every door rattled, the resonance made weird noises on both stained and plain glass windows. The oscillations of those notes seemed to vibrate the pews.

The one thing she was afraid of was thunder, and Bunch would arrange to have someone for company when thunder was forecast. It was quite an honour to stay overnight at her cottage. As the thunder rumbled over the Cotswolds and the lightning made daylight in the Vale, Bunch would sit under the stairs with her companion. Here they would eat cold chicken and salad and drink Bulmer's Woodpecker cider.

She was a good cook and a dedicated gardener. Often have I seen her kitchen sink piled high with washing up until all the crocks had been used except her best pieces in the china cabinet. Bunch had been gardening from morning until night and when the weather broke she washed up. A happy spinster who made no secret of the fact she was in love with her doctor.

Her garden was the village as well as her enclosure. On grassy banks she planted daffodils, she planted shrubs in our rickyard. As I lit a bonfire of rubbish in the rickyard corner and saw Bunch come running across the road I wondered why. 'You are burning my broom, you young monkey.'

'Where's the broom, Miss Baldwyn?' I replied, not seeing a broom among the flames.

'My broom bush, you've burnt it,' she replied. The feeling that one of Bunch's efforts to beautify the village had been destroyed left me speechless until I said quietly, 'I'm so sorry, Miss Baldwyn,' not knowing a broom shrub from a hawthorn bush.

For years a state of friendly rivalry existed between Bunch and Harold Wigley; Harold was brother-in-law to the vicar and spent his time keeping what he called, God's acre, the churchyard, tidy. Harold did two things which annoyed Bunch. He kept stocking away at the grass verges of the churchyard path. Every year the path grew wider until Bunch told him that there would soon be room for a charabanc to travel that way. Harold treated her with great respect but got a bit tired of being told that she had more bones in the churchyard than he had. He turfed some double graves with such high mounds that Bunch called them marrow beds.

In Bunch's garden stood a statue of a beautiful woman. Harold, a paragon of politeness, never failed to raise his trilby hat to Miss Bunch Baldwyn. In the gathering gloom of a November evening Harold looked across Bunch's garden and thought he recognized her, but it was the marble image. Bunch stood in fits of laughter at her back door when Harold raised his hat to the statue saying, 'Good night, Miss Baldwyn.'

Mr Frank Field came from nearby Sedgeberrow to farm what was known as Manor Farm. He was the son of Mr Henry Field of Evesham who had been until his death early in life a legendary character in the market gardening world. Frank and his wife, affectionately known as 'Lady Maud', lived in an Elizabethan house with an impressive entrance drive where two great stone balls topped the gateway.

A man of faith, one time church warden, he was always working and scheming, while Lady Maud was a benefactor to the poor. She rivalled Bunch Baldwyn in good works. She dressed rather grand – her cast-offs clothed many of the poorer women of the village. There was a graciousness about this lady who would have been quite at home at a royal garden party. Frank was a great believer in early co-operative farming. In a small way it did operate in the 'twenties; in the farming fraternity implements were borrowed, horses leant to smallholders, and men hired at busy times from farmer to farmer. This lending and borrowing of implements did cause amusement at farm sales. As some farmers failed in the Depression years on the land and went bankrupt, their neighbours sometimes found implements of theirs numbered in the lines of dead stock to be auctioned, sending their carters and horses to reclaim ploughs and waggons in the nick of time.

Mr Frank Field kept a useful herd of Shorthorn cows. He and his cowman milked them by hand, but Frank was the only man I ever saw who smoked cigarettes as he milked from the stool with a reversed greasy cap on his head. The dairy in Birmingham, Wates, Gattel and Gurden, complained of finding something odd in the milk: cigarette ash from Frank's Gold Flake. Frank just smiled at this little error, but waited until after milking to enjoy his smokes thereafter.

Frank was one of those who struggled through the Depression years of the 'twenties and 'thirties, living on very little more than the cheap labourers he employed. Humour was one of Frank Field's invaluable assets. He employed a chap who lived in a tumbledown cottage way out in a field. A man who had tramped the roads, a heavy drinker who was given the job of re-making a field fence with the conventional withy poles and stakes. Frank looked at this man's efforts in making the field stock proof. The fence was six feet high, the stakes uneven; a very untidy job. 'It's to keep cows in, Arthur, this isn't a deer park. Still, I suppose it will frighten them, and they do say the rougher the better.'

Sidney Wesley Church was an impeccably dressed dentist who drove a smart car. He changed his car yearly for a new one, a very rare thing in the 'twenties. He practised in Evesham, belonged to the Gentleman's Club, yet was a good friend to the working man. Mr Church would often be disturbed from his Sunday afternoon nap by some poor chap mad with toothache. Sidney pulled out the offending tooth, sometimes on his lawn outside his house.

'How much, sir?' would get the reply, 'Oh, that's alright, George.' But Sidney was often rewarded by a punnet of strawberries or a cauliflower left on the doorstep by the cottage.

The second social stratum of the village was the backbone of country life; the top layer was fertile, prosperous, but softer, and, like different layers of rock, the lower levels were often harder. They were older, submerged by the passage of time and weather, but supporting the other seams. Some of these families were mentioned in the Enclosure Award of 1783. A few had retained their freehold while others had been absorbed by the landowners.

Here we had the village post master and shopkeeper, Mr Fred Tandy, and his wife; dependable, honest trade folk supplying, apart from the postal service, the immediate wants of the village from washing soda and boiled sweets to Carter's tested seeds. He and his wife manned the little telephone exchange from the outset when only ten houses had a 'phone. There were benefits from having a manually operated exchange for once we were ringing one of the ten subscribers and Fred volunteered the useful information that it was no good ringing for a while, for the gentleman's car was parked outside The Star Inn.

In times past news was gathered and exchanged at the blacksmith's shop, but when the phone came to the post office, it was an information bureau where the state of a parishioner's health could be gleaned, the demand for produce at the local market, the fire engine from Evesham going to a rick fire, or why the trains were running late on our little branch line. Fred, however, was a diplomat, careful not to divulge lots of little secrets passing along the wires.

Mr Boucher was porter in charge at our railway station. It seemed that our station didn't quite warrant a station master. We were under Beckford, where cattle could be loaded, a superior village with a signal box alongside the line. If someone in Ashton got a bit knowing he would soon be told, 'Thee hast bin to Beckford,' for the parson and the policeman lived there and there at one time at the Court House Petty Sessions were held.

Mr Boucher had a porter under him to deliver telegrams and help to load the goods trucks, to bowl the seventeen gallon milk churns to platform two across the level crossing. Mr Boucher was essentially a company man, loyal to the Midland Railway. During the 1926 General Strike he still worked for the company. As a boy I was afraid of him at times. His uniform, his clipped moustache, gave him authority.

Ray, his understudy, used to load the goods trucks when Bert our drayman took sprouts to load in hampers for Nottingham, Manchester, Chesterfield, Leeds and Liverpool. Ray checked the numbers of packages. He opened the heavy doors of the goods waggons and collected the consignment notes while Mr Boucher sat in the booking office listening for the morse code bleeps from the telegraph wires, issued the pasteboard tickets, supervising.

It was always hot in winter in the booking office. The glowing stove, the desk, the office chair, gave it the appearance of a comfortable den. When Ray was up in the village delivering parcels or telegrams Mr Boucher was loath to leave his little office and face the wind, the rain, the snow and do the labouring job of loading the goods trucks. It was important to use tact when currying a favour.

When the milk float took the churns to catch the 8.10 train they were loaded onto a four-wheeled trolley. It took two men to push the load up the incline past the level crossing to platform two. Mr Boucher would delay until the little tank engine was on its way from Hinton. Then a rush with the trolley across the lines as the engine approached the station.

Mr Boucher was certainly a company man. He kept the station immaculately clean, his garden tidy. By the weighbridge with its little hut built like the station house in soft blue ligstone, was a well fenced orchard of pear trees. Here Mr Boucher kept a flock of Light Sussex hens and some pigs. It always seemed completely daft to me that when a churn of milk was gone off, turned sour in the summer sun, it was returned from the dairy in Birmingham. This thick custard-like seventeen gallons was fed to Mr Boucher's pigs, then the churn was scalded and sent back on the float to our farm.

My first venture at loading produce by rail with a dray was a load of Warner King apples for Nottingham. Pleasant the dray mare was nervous of smoke and steam from the shunting engine. Trying my best to draw the dray alongside the goods waggon with Pleasant with ears laid back and pottering about the goods yard was anything but successful. 'That's near enough,' Mr Boucher said in desperation, the dray being a couple of yards away from the truck and Mr Boucher impatient, waiting at the door of the goods waggon. I carried twenty-five hampers of apples from the dray while he stacked them in the truck for Nottingham. 'Bring a steadier horse next time, Fred, just tell your Dad.' I gave him the consignment note and he invited me into his office for a cup of tea.

It was a fact in those days that men in charge of railway stations had to be treated with respect. Bert and Mr Boucher never seemed to see eye to eye. One day Bert had to wait for him to load a truck and he threatened to report him to Derby. Out of a drawer came a complaint form which was thrust into Bert's hand. 'There,' he said, 'fill that in and send it to Derby.' Bert was so scared he ripped the form up on his way back to the farm. 'Report Master Boucher to Derby,' he told me, 'he's a company man, and he and your Dad are friends.'

Mr Boucher was held in great respect but would not be dictated to by farm labourers. I was always particular to respect him; it paid to. He allowed me to pick up the windfall pears when I came home from school on the 4.05 train and he would weigh me on the waiting room machine, and sometimes give me telegrams to deliver to Dad.

How did you take the step onto the bottom but one rung of the social ladder? The men on farm and market garden first of all would buy for a few pounds the fruit in a retired gentleman's garden. Evenings in summer found them with a ladder picking apples and plums, then stacking their produce outside their cottage doors to be picked up for market by Harry Stratford's

lorry. He returned with the empty boxes, crates and even collected their returns on Saturdays at the market. A few pounds, a few shillings. Here was an enterprise where the little money snowballed in a good year but gave disappointment in a bad year. Little was at stake and the weekly thirty shillings paid by the farmer was their wage.

On the allotment land men grew sprouts for picking on Saturday afternoons in winter. After years of intense thrift a man could maybe work three days on a farm and three days on his own smallholding; then he would rent more smallholding land from the county council, and finally leave the farm and be independent.

It's often been said that it's hard after years as an employee to become one's own master: drought, flood, hard winters and bad prices are the nightmare of the little master man. In this interesting group of family men struggling to exist much was accomplished by muscle power. They pulled their little harrows, pushed their seed drills, their wives picked the peas, tied the spring onions. Some men fell by the wayside during the Depression years, while others prospered. The survival of the fittest in some ways, but so often the smallholdings were on difficult land. The art of working the clay was vital. Strong men like Alfred Grove wheeled his produce to the railway station on a flat bottomed Evesham barrow to get a few extra shillings from the markets of the north. Others like William Sandford and Tom Hunting had a pony and dray.

The Vale of Evesham blossomed as the plums in April with scores of these folk. Not since before the Enclosures had small acreages been tilled, not to grow wheat for the bread oven as then, but to give colour and variety to the countryside and market. Produce from the holdings, hand sown, hand picked, realized a little more per package than the bigger growers'. Loving care from seedtime to harvest could never be given by the piece-work men employed over the hedge.

It's wrong to group farm labourers into just one category. A definite sub-division was in existence in our village. Orders would be given to the hoers, the fruit pickers, under cowmen or draymen (who form my fourth class), but never to the shepherd. He would be consulted by the farmer at every stage of the farming calendar. Shepherd Tidmarsh was a law unto himself. His experience and wisdom was consulted in the choice of rams at tupping time. He chose the sheep dips, he said how much cotton cake was mixed with linseed cake. He decided when it was safe to feed mangolds to the ewes. He culled the broken-mouthed ewes from the flock. Dad would not say, shear the sheep, dip the sheep, wean the lambs, but, 'Do you think, shepherd, it's time to do these things?' and the shepherd's timing was always right. Shepherd Tidmarsh was waited on at busy times but helped in the hayfield when he could spare a few hours from the flock. He had to be asked to come, not told. His work was appreciated.

The carter, who did the horse ploughing, cultivating, planting and harvesting, also had status. Ralph Pratt used which horses he wanted and left the less handy ones for odd jobs. The horses he referred to as 'my 'osses'. He would be consulted whether to use the heavy scuffle or the duck foot drags to make a tilth for the planting. 'I want some fittle or vittels for my osses' was a statement to be recognized by the farmer. Sometimes the farmer would skimp the horse fodder and Ralph, like all good carters, would fetch corn from the granary allocated for the sheep and feed his horses.

Tom the cowman weaned calves, turned out the cattle from the yards in May when he thought it right. Again, no labourer, but a skilled man with the worker's participation in management.

One didn't tell Jack Hunting, that man of so many parts, how to lay a hedge, drain a field, make a gate or ladder, mend a fence, make a shaft for a horse rake or any of the maintenance jobs on the land. He kept oak, ash and larch seasoning in his workshop to make or mend almost anything. He knew that red withy made ladder rungs, ash made shafts, split withy was for mending fences.

The ordinary labourers were skilled men, but not specialists. They worked in a gang, receiving less money and sweating long hours in the hayfield. Then they did piece work. Men did struggle to exist on thirty shillings per week [£1.50] even on low house rents of three shillings [15p] per week. Those with higher rents were in real trouble. Poverty in the village was not as bad as in the town. There was always something to be gathered in season: vegetables, the potato headland, blackberries for market, mushrooms, all within the scope of the enterprising farm worker. He had his pig, his apple tree, and he worked overtime; yet if the basic wage had been raised by as little as five shillings per week he would have been more comfortable.

The worst off were the widows and the pensioners. When a man and wife each drew ten shillings [50p] per week (pension) they could manage, but when one died and the income fell to one pension of ten shillings per week, the partner left behind was poor, very poor. The Guardian's Committee, of which Dad was a member, would give relief, but not very much. Some pensioners called it 'going on the Parish'. They had pride and there was a stigma to 'going on the Parish'. The workhouse was a thing which elderly people dreaded, especially an aged couple who had to be parted.

And so the last pieces in the jigsaw complete the picture of a village at work in the 'twenties. Which piece would I have chosen to be a tiny part of the puzzle had I not been the second son of a fairly big farmer? The piece in that jigsaw I would not have liked to be can be said without hesitation. It sounds progressive to be one of the little master men, but that wouldn't have been my choice. They were the hardest workers, toiling relentlessly for long hours with no guarantee of a return. They are a class I admired, with broad shoulders, a strong backbone, and, as Alfred Grove once said, like Elijah having to be fed by the ravens.

No, it would have been the role of Shepherd Tidmarsh, the monarch of the sheep. He made his wine, grew his potatoes and beans in the garden and when he killed a 'teg', or yearling sheep, to be divided among the men, they paid for their joints, but the shepherd had the pluck (liver, etc.) as a bonus. His unhurried life on the hill, having time to stand and stare, I envied. You see, a galloping shepherd is no good for his master or the sheep. He must stand, stare, assess, evaluate, ruminate, think.

Education didn't play such a role as today. In fact the folk who farmed the cattle and sheep, grew the crops, looked on it as a hindrance, saying so often, 'You can't farm from a book.' This was the day of the horse and simple tackle when the land was fed by hoof and horn, by farmyard muck, and sprays and chemicals were not in use. Education was knowing the land, knowing when to buy, when to sell, when to plant and harvest; to recognize a good horse, a good beef or milk cow, a stock ram. There were few forms to fill in. Butchers bought cattle by what was known as the scowl of brow, in fact by feel, estimating dressed carcass weight before weighing machines were in the markets.

Simple arithmetic and a good hand with the pen were about all that was needed to learn how to farm or how to work on a farm. Saints Days on the calendar told men when to plant and harvest; farmers jokingly said that when a new baby was born the carter would have to plough one more furrow under the hedge to grow a little more of the crops. If classes there must be, the system I've described, though not ideal, was much better than a pattern of competitiveness.

CHAPTER FIVE

School

PREP SCHOOL

A few weeks before my fifth birthday I joined my brother Tom at Evesham Preparatory School. Wearing uniform softened the blow for the great adventure; to travel on the Midland Railway the five miles morning and afternoon from our station was to go to another county.

Mother had spent the best part of a day with me at Lloyd's the tailors buying the cap, new grey shorts, long socks and a navy blazer with the legend EPS in bright red and a cap to match with an enormous badge. Then to Huin's the shoe-shop where Mr Clews fitted me up with a pair of black lace-up shoes. Ever since I had seen cousin Tom in his khaki and fingered the brass buttons of his tunic, I had been entranced by uniforms.

A kind young lady named Gladys who had filled the shells for the cannons of war now worked as a dressmaker in town. She shepherded us the half mile to the station from the farm and travelled with us in those red and black upholstered carriages of the Midland Railway. The train was packed with business folk and shoppers. The step up off the platform to the third class compartment was quite a challenge. Gladys allowed me to move the little lever above the seat and put the heating off and on, heating from the steam of the boiler of the little tank engine with long funnels which sometimes pulled us, sometimes pushed us from behind. On the step a band of polished brass was just a part of that steam heating system. Independent of Gladys I put my hand on the step and burnt it slightly on the hot flat pipe. A huge whiskered farmer from the station before ours dried my tears in a red spotted handkerchief and gave me a humbug.

The High Street rattled with the iron wheels of market gardener's drays drawn by fast nags, railway drays drawn by massive Shire horses, horses bigger than the farm horses, horses without blinkers. They plodded at our pace with loads of merchandise for the shops. Sleek they were with polished brasses. Little bells rang from their bridles. Men on coal drays were black-faced as the coal. From the back axles of their drays nosebags of corn and chaff swung to and fro at every step.

Miss Morris the head teacher greeted her new pupils in the cloakroom where we hung our satchels on a row of hooks near her bicycle: a bicycle which she had suspended from the ceiling on two leather straps to preserve the rubber tyres, by keeping them off the red flagstone floor. Miss Morris conducted prayers in the music room where she played the piano for the morning hymn. 'There is a green hill far away without a city wall,' confused me. Why wasn't there a city wall? Walls enclosed the fields on the hill; one enclosed the churchyard. Then we recited the Catechism which included, 'I believe in the Holy Catholic church.' Not for me the Catholic church, for hadn't we been told that the Pope's teaching was all wrong?

The infants' classroom on the first floor of that old town house was my first experience of book learning. Miss Norledge guided my hand with a pencil to make pot hooks. Her little class, all boys, had to perfect pot hooks before the ABC was taught. These pencilled Js and undotted Is were great fun. The chalked emblems on the blackboard didn't resemble my first efforts.

We had lunch in the big room, Miss Morris's room, where the mature students learnt the three Rs and French. Three rows of desks in line stood facing a tiled fireplace. The ceiling of the room reminded me of a palace: fancy cornices went in squares from the walls, squares which became smaller, finishing in the middle where the gas lamp hung on brackets from the ceiling. A picture of Kitchener in all his khaki and brass hung over the door, while a multi-antlered stag in a framed oil painting called 'The Monarch of the Glen' hung by the side of the white painted French window.

From the desk, as the banana sandwiches and the Camp Coffee bottle of cold tea provided lunch, I looked out to a different world from the village. The playground was hemmed by tall brick walls, the walls of shops and houses. Two swings hung on plough traces like chains, too big for a five-year-old, reminding me of gibbets I'd seen in pictures of the old days on the Cotswolds. I dared not go near them that first playtime, but watched with Billy Lunn who was a little older than me but was in Miss Norledge's class. I watched the big boys swing high as the chains creaked from the hangings.

Miss Morris rang a bell when the mealtime was over. She was a kind lady, rather fat, and wore a sort of riding habit skirt and only the string dress guard on her cycle prevented it from being entangled in the spokes of the back wheel when she mounted what was known as a sit-up-and-beg green-painted Sunbeam bike.

Trudging tired to the station at a quarter to four we crossed the branch line by the bridge. In fifteen minutes the tank engine stopped at our station where we crossed the line by the level crossing. Mr Boucher the porter in charge saw us safely over. I remember the plate layers dressed in sleeved waistcoats and cord trousers wielding their sledge hammers and driving the wedges home into what were known as the chairs which held the metals on the permanent way. The ganger, a heavy weatherbeaten man, said his usual piece.

'Had the cane today?'

'No,' I replied.

'Well, you ought to have done, 'cos I know you deserve it.' He had a very strong voice which carried and when the men were carrying sleepers he'd call, 'Your way a bit, Joby.'

My season ticket, sewed by Mother on the inside of my blazer, had to be shown at the town station. We called, 'Season.' The ticket collector let us through but Mr Boucher at our village station knew us as we passed through the booking office there on our way home.

Mother always cooked at midday so our late dinner was in the oven. The potatoes had gone a bit brown, the cabbage a bit sad, the meat was either beef or lamb for Mother didn't believe in pork. Then we finished with rice, tapioca or sago skimmed over in the dish from the oven.

Every week Miss Morris came to look at our work in the infants class. The desks held two children so when Miss Morris sat beside me and guided my hand sitting down, room was restricted. Her hair was combed back off her forehead, her face heavily powdered and scented, her breath giving away a secret she tried to keep from us boys, for she smoked, but not at school. I thought her daring. She smoked little Jersey Lily cigarettes so Billy Lunn told me when she went to his mother's house in the evenings.

The school was a happy place, for she was in constant touch with parents, so eager was she that everyone be both happy and learning their lessons. Two canes hung in the store room where the exercise books, pens and pencils were kept. One a pale yellow bamboo with a handle like a walking stick, the other straight, brown, like a slender round ruler. She rarely used them but did cane Billy Lunn and me for fighting and coming from the playground with bloody noses.

One lunch-time when I watched her bank the fire up with wet slack coal, it almost went out. She took a double sheet from an old copy of *The Times* and put it in front to draw the fire, telling us boys never to do such a thing as it was dangerous. She used to read to us from *The Times*, the cricket scores from the Test Matches in Australia in those pre-wireless days, every morning after prayers. A keen follower of cricket she was, and if Hobbs and Sutcliffe had done well she was in a happy mood all day.

Across the yard from the cloakroom door was a whitewashed stone floored wash house: one brass tap over a brown crock sink and a roller towel. This roller towel, red-and-white striped, was another plaything for a boy in the infants' class. Never had I seen such a contraption, an endless supply of towelling to wipe our hands on. I pulled it around and around at playtime, the unfurling of a flag, the raising of the sails on a ship. Miss Morris kept a stock of Lifebuoy soap and told us, 'Cleanliness is next to Godliness.'

The adjoining building housed the WC, so modern, so different from the earth closet at home. How the rushing water roared its way from the high cistern and why was there always some water left in the white crock pan was a mystery. A lead overflow pipe stuck out of the brick wall like the barrel of a gun. By using the lead pipe lever-like when a classmate was inside, the cistern rocked; off-putting to the inmate. I suppose this pipe had been levered up and down by the pupils for maybe years. Why was it that I broke it off the wall? Miss Morris looked very grave when she knew that the cistern's exhaust had been broken by me and gave me a sealed envelope to take home to my parents. Dad was a great believer in instant punishment, the reduction in pocket money never appealed to him. Mother was so different for she would bring up my wrongdoings over and over again. As Dad read the note I knew what the punishment would be. He unbuckled his broad leather belt and put me across his knee and the strap stung through my flannel shorts, wasp like. The bill came a week later, seventeen shillings and six pence. A new lead pipe took the place of the broken overflow, never again to be touched by me.

The school observed a whole string of Saints Days, when we marched to All Saints Church. Here was a grand edifice of christianity where the slight smell of incense cloaked the musty smell of history. Miss Morris thundered the great organ and we sat there with Miss Norledge observing the martyrdom of some saint or other.

From Northfield Cripples Hospital every pupil had a Cripple Box to put pennies in for the crippled children. By putting into the box a little more than a halfpenny [¼p] a week, the boxes when emptied yearly yielded half a crown [12½p]. By giving half a crown we were decorated with a little badge and given a bar of Callard and Bowsers butterscotch. Miss Wildblood came from Birmingham and emptied the boxes on the table by the fire. She talked to us about the work among the cripples. As I listened the whole subject of cripples escaped my mind. Miss Wildblood's appearance made my eyes just boggle, my mouth open wide. A tall lady, taller than Miss Morris, she stood by the fire, auburn hair done neatly in a bob with a curved celluloid comb.

Wildblood did seem to suit this lovely lady for her neck above the line of her blouse flushed as red as sunset. The whole wave of red rose like a threatening red sunrise to her chin, then her cheeks, and I was afraid. Little did I know that hot flushes were the bane of some middle-aged ladies. No one told me and I dared not ask. Perhaps no one else noticed.

Although school in a little market town, alive with the clatter of dray wheels, the clip clop of horses, the braying of donkeys in the fruit market, was only five miles from Fred Randall's and the cows on the farm, it was like a different world.

Miss Morris did instil into my young mind a love of cricket. She marched us down every Wednesday past Espleys saw mills to the river meadow and here she umpired the game. It was a hot summer's day when a big boy was batting, I think it was Bert Haines. Miss Morris, apart from being umpire, set the field and put me fairly close at short leg. Bert gave an almighty swipe. The ball came to me head high, but, muffing the catch, it hit me fair and square on the brow. The stars shone as I crumpled to the grass. A walnut sized lump soon made a little promontory on my brow. Miss Morris picked me up and from her handbag applied fresh farm butter to the damaged part. What a lady, having butter at a cricket match, and then she consulted Bert the batsman saying, 'Freddy made a great effort for a catch. Shall we say you are out? Please yourself, Bert, how do you feel?' Bert came to me and helped to dry the tears and the score card read, caught Archer, bowled Lunn. The cricket field by the river appealed to me for it was a boy's ambition to kick a ball into that sedgy banked Avon where the dragonflies dipped over the water.

An hour for midday lunch is much too long to eat a banana sandwich and drink a bottle of tea. With a bent pin on a piece of pudding string and a withy stick, Billy and I fished, caught gudgeon and minnow with bread paste. The mysterious Glover's Island lay like a long green willow-covered no man's land. When the water was low it was accessible, for Dad once grazed a pony there, but it was an eerie place between the meadow and Clark's Hill. Near here the ferryman pulled his boat to and fro with a rope which joined Evesham to Hampton.

One of the boys in my class was the son of a High Church vicar. He brought to school those little purple pyramids of incense and gave me a couple. It was Sunday dinnertime, Sunday best suit covered with a white apron and the family sat around while the joint was carved. I had lit the incense under the piano. 'Something burning,' Dad said, putting down the carving knife. The grey smoke filled the room, Mother carried the offending thing on a coal shovel and tipped it on the courtyard. A couple of smacks from Dad and when dinner was resumed he and Mother both laughed.

GRAMMAR SCHOOL

The year was 1926, the year of the General Strike, when I started at Prince Henry's Grammar school at Evesham. When the trains stopped running on the little branch line it meant cycling the six miles to town. Quite a pleasant exercise in summer, seeing the market gardeners working alongside the main road and stacks of bundled asparagus and chips of strawberries on the roadside verge awaiting the carrier's cart for market. School had always been so happy a place under Miss Morris, a kind discipline when we were guided along certain well worn paths of behaviour without a thought of questioning the validity of the course.

At John Lloyds, the official outfitter for PHGS, Dad fitted me with the necessary uniform to start in form 2B. Miss Lamshead the teacher was a kind lady, her hair done in two plaits known as earphones. This did not affect her hearing. She wore a black band of ribbon around her neck and was very keen on nature study. This suited me for when specimens were needed I could supply moles, rabbits, hedgehogs and some rare plants which grew on Bredon Hill. I got on fine with Miss Lamshead, but in the strawberry season I took strawberries to school every day. A Blue Bird toffee tin would just hold a pound punnet of fruit. This was a must in my satchel. I sat in the back row next to a straight-haired Eton-cropped girl named Betty. We polished off a pound of strawberries daily when Miss Lamshead's back was turned.

Then it happened. The teacher sat at my desk and corrected an essay with her red-inked pen and suddenly said, 'I smell strawberries.' Blushingly I replied, 'Can you, Miss Lamshead?'

'Now then, where are they?' she said sternly and opened the desk lid and there among the textbooks a half eaten tin of fruit, best Royal Sovereigns, was the indisputable evidence. She took the tin to her desk and I never saw it again; I was given fifty lines to write, 'I must not eat strawberries in class.'

But life in 2B with Miss Lamshead was similar to being at the prep school with Miss Morris. Nature walks along the River Avon banks where we caught dragonflies; longing for the outdoors instead of the great radiator-heated, feet-smelling hall at the school, I counted the months until the release at sixteen years old. I did fairly well for a couple of years and then, after a grumbling appendix and operation, fell from second in the class to bottom, and then never caught up; I then just longed to get away to the land.

The School Certificate exam was as usual in July. I knew the teachers thought that I'd never pass, and persuaded Dad to let me leave the previous Christmas. Dad tried his best to get me to stay and take the exam, adding I was valuable to him for his Income Tax.

The last day at Prince Henry's was unforgettable. Three of us left that Christmas and said our farewells in the Doctor's (the headmaster's) office. Over his desk a very good line drawing of him hung in a black frame with these words underneath, 'The Doctor's Dilemma'. If only Shaw had known the truth about him.

For the first time in five years I stood there unafraid of him. His black-booted feet were on the mantlepiece above the fireplace. He was smoking a rather long, ebony coloured pipe, his acid stained gown wrapped around him like a sleeping bag. The term was over, he was relaxed and so was I. After warning us of wine and women, he then said, 'Don't ever start smoking.' The little office was full of tobacco smoke. 'Why do you think I'm smoking, Archer?' Not knowing the answer to that, I awaited his reply which came directly. 'The same reason as I wear my boots – habit,' he said. 'Don't get into bad habits.'

'Now, Archer, what are you going to do now you are leaving school?' to which I answered, 'I'm going to be a farmer, sir.'

'Well you will have to farm with your feet because you have got no brains,' he replied.

FARM LABOURER

The December day when two or three of us bade farewell to the headmaster was a redletter day in my life, as if a two hundredweight sack of corn had been shed from my shoulders.

The school hall was packed with four hundred pupils for the breaking up ceremony and we all sang, 'Lord dismiss us with Thy blessing'; I took my bike from the bike shed and rode down the High Street. The policeman at the Town Hall waved me through the Market Square.

That winter was severe. The snow began before Christmas. Dad said, 'You really aught to have gone in for a parson.' Mr Bailey his partner added, 'Fred doesn't care whether the cow calves or the bull breaks his neck.' But I did want to learn; not the book knowledge of Prince Henry's, but to learn what life was all about among the crops and cattle on the hill, in the market. Education was to begin in earnest.

As the frost made the sprout leaves droop every morning, silvering the green, concreting the land, the wood pigeons hungry for food came in hordes. Their numbers were multiplied by the flocks of birds from Scandinavia. Our men pushed the bullet-hard green buds of sprouts into forty pound hampers. They shivered over a bait-time fire. The outlying cattle stood by the gate, hungry for hay. Winter came hard and cruel.

Dad warned me, 'You will have to do your shot.' Later I learnt that a shot was a strip of land, a portion. At Taffy Johns's Army and Navy Stores I bought a pair of tarpaulin over trousers and joined the sprout pickers with Frank, my sixteen-year-old friend. We blew warm air into our frozen hands, clapped our arms and picked sprouts. Our fingers burned with cold, our backs ached and old Uncle George called us 'The Specials'. I watched George, the best picker, carry hamper after hamper to the weighing scales and thought of the radiators in the stuffy, often sweat-smelling, classrooms of the grammar school.

After tea in the oil-lit farmhouse it was heaven by the fireside with the horned loudspeaker of the wireless set telling us the news, news apart from the local *Echo*. Then music. Mabel Constanduros and Grandma Leonard Henry. Evening fireside concerts and no homework.

Thirty cattle lay on Spring Hill by Great Hill barn. The gully up the cart track was filled with snow. In the field with the cattle Turpin the chocolate coloured gelding shared their hay and I was sent with Tom the cowman to help him fodder the outliers. Tom climbed the ladder, cut the kerves of hay and I loaded the cart from the rick. We made a line of hay from the cart in the snow, then unhooked Turpin and turned him out among his horned companions. This was better than picking sprouts and Tom kept up a continual stream of wit and wisdom as we walked down the hill. From the hill top we could see a line of bent men sprout-picking in Beckford's Way.

Another field of sprouts looked frosted and sad over Great Hill wall. The pigeons were there in hordes. I told Dad how the pigeons were ragging the crop, then Mr Bailey gave me a box of cartridges and his gun and sent me up there early next morning. Being up there early, I'd be able to help Tom with the foddering of the cattle about lunchtime at ten o'clock.

Blazing away with Mr Bailey's twelve-bore gun and dropping a few birds down among the sprout rows earned me twelve shillings [60p] a week, and made me feel important, a cog in the chain of men and boys.

Mr Bailey came one morning and together we built a hide, or what the locals called a 'cave', of hawthorn branches and larch poles under a Cotswold-type wall. We covered it with brush or small wood until it was wigwamlike. Here, sitting on a pot hamper, I was able to shoot the birds as they settled on the sprout tops from the Grafton firs. As they rose like a cloud of silver and blue, two barrels of number four shot from Mr Bailey's gun would kill some and frighten the others away. Cosy in the hide with food to eat and a bottle of tea to drink, and no one to tell me, do this, do that, was like being a solitary ruler of the hill.

Every day when the four o'clock dusk fell I took a bag of birds home and met Mr Bailey in the yard. As I tipped out my bag in front of him he laughed and said, 'Do you want more cartridges?' (They were two pence [1p] each.) From the dairy he gave me another lot of ammunition. 'Try these, Fred, I got them cheap off Mr Barrat.' I opened the boxes and there were a mixture of cartridges with black rings around the cases and charged with black powder. 'That will put fear into the varmints,' he said, and sure enough the smoke from the powder and the loud report of the gun gave me a feeling of some ancient gamekeeper, but I found them not so deadly as the number four shot crimson flash. They were more for scaring than killing.

My next task was to wait on Mr Bailey and Jack Hunting, trapping and wiring rabbits. I carried the snares and with a little home-made mallet knocked in the pegs which held the wires. The mallet was made of crab apple wood with an ash handle. Mr Bailey set his snares twice as fast as Jack, for Jack was an older man, but canny, for on the night time trek on the hill with George collecting the snared rabbits I noticed that most of Jack's snares held a bunny. I loved snaring rabbits. It seemed pretty humane as we took them from their necklaces at night by the light of a carbide bicycle lamp.

Gin trapping (a spring trap) I detested. It was cruel and besides that a messy job trowelling the fine earth over the pedal-like part of the trap between the ugly jaws. It also meant scrabbling under hedges where the rabbit holes were among the thorns. I remember the rattle of the trap's chain when a rabbit was in the trap and so often taking the little animal out with a broken leg.

The sounds of the hill in winter – the call of the dog fox, the scream of the vixen, the note of whistling plovers overhead – were nature as I knew it under the moon and stars at night. The hill was lonely, but beautiful.

The rabbitting on the hill was over in February when the does were in kindle. Vegetable prices were so bad that often the rabbit money helped to pay the men's wages. One of the trials experienced by Mr Bailey in circling the hill with snares was a badger which lay in a holt on a bank called Morrisons. Every night he would steal his supper from our snares. It interested me how he would paunch and skin a rabbit and leave that behind. Mr Bailey set four gin traps at the mouth of his holt and sprinkled some fine soil over the trap pedal. We never caught him. It's said they will roll over on their back and let traps off before making their exit. I do know they are very clever.

One night under a February moon and a starlit sky I walked with Dad and Monty his black spaniel from Grafton Coppice where we had been pigeon shooting. It was here the birds came to roost with their bloated sprout-filled crops. We stood among the ivy under the tall poplar trees and listened for the flop of their wings as they settled. In the dusk the hordes of birds dive-bombed the coppice then cooed to each other, a satisfying, full bellied noise. Taking aim with my single barrelled converted bolt action rifle I dropped the first bird among the greening kingcups underfoot, a swampy eerie coppice on the hillside. Dad would bag a couple, left and right barrels, and Monty retrieved.

I reckon Dad loved Monty next to Mother and Tom, Clarice

(my sister) and me. They were seldom apart.

As we walked silently along the brow of Quar Hill and by the big elder hedge over into Morrisons, Monty was nosing for rabbits along the hedge bottom warrens. Suddenly we heard a cry of pain from Monty. He cried like a child. We dropped our guns and down by the withy fence there was Monty with three of his legs trapped in the gin traps at the mouth of the badger holt. One trap remained still set.

Dad let it off with a stick then put his foot on the sprung handle of each trap while one by one in the moonlight Monty's feet were freed. He picked up his dog in his arms and loved him like a baby. It seemed that the whimpering of the black spaniel said his thank you.

My father was an even tempered man. It took a lot to rouse him but that night I sensed that his rosy face would be white with rage. I waited. We never spoke until he said, 'Oh, I wish that Harry would not set traps in the open.' One at a time he held the chains of the gins and threw them to the bottom of Morrisons bank.

We called on Mr Harry Bailey and he was sorry about Monty, but fortunately none of the dog's legs were broken. 'I'll catch that badger, Tom.'

The next day I watched Jack Hunting spin a snare from strands of steel wire and went with him in the evening to Morrisons bank and here he set a snare anchored to an elder stool. It was Sunday morning when Mr Bailey found Brock with his necklace on, grunting and threatening us at the mouth of the holt. The most humane way to kill a badger is to shoot it. 'Ah, Fred, I reckon Arthur Cross may like to shoot the badger. I'll give him a ring.'

Mr Cross, a solicitor from Evesham, arrived and despatched the rabbit-eating native of the hill and Jack Hunting skinned it for him.

As a boy, two things I remember about paunching rabbits. Firstly how deftly Mr Bailey could do this. With a sharp penknife he would paunch and hock forty rabbits in a few minutes and if we wanted one for dinner he would crack their jaws between finger and thumb. A young rabbit's jaws cracked easily so he'd say. 'Here you are, take this to your Mother.' I also recall how potent the smell of disembowelled rabbits was and how it impregnated the system so that the day after on breaking wind the strong rabbit smell would be an unpleasant incense in the house.

Dad was intent that I should learn more of the cattle side of work on the farm; I suppose I learnt more from Tom Whittle, our stockman, than anyone. You see he was a teacher, for when he tackled any job he would say, 'Now watch what I be doing, 'cos one day you'll have to take over.' To learn the ways of handling cattle was fascinating and soon he would let me do certain things. A calf in the top shed must be drenched for scour. He handed me what he called a puff-hugh powder, mostly chalk, and with a small bottle I drenched the scouring calf.

Something was always cropping up. We had a beast with wooden tongue, then the yearlings had husk. No vet was called, Tom could cope. Weaned calves were grazed on Parkers Hill where the keep was sparse, rather than the lush pasture of the Leasows. Rich grass would bloat young calves.

Life with Tom was the best education anyone could wish for. I liked to see him drive the hay knife into a rick and cut square kerves of the sweet smelling fodder and carry it to the yarded cattle. It was a whiff of summer, that perfume of June in February. A cut, as it was known, in a rick, was about a yard square, so as the rick was started from the eaves to the staddle it stood there as a golden cottage well upright and straight. The next cut began farther up the face of the hayrick, another tightly packed square, matured like tobacco, yet sweet as honey. After the section of thatch had been taken off and the straw used for litter, the rick pegs stacked by me in the barn for yet another year, Tom used a smaller hay knife to start a cut, a lighter one, to carry up the ladder. Then he drove the big knife, sharpened by a blue whetstone, vertically into the hay, cutting a mattress a foot deep, and with a hayfork pitched it to the rickyard floor.

Tom was a gentle man, always the same except some Saturday afternoons when Tom Baldwyn's cider made him what was known as 'conterairey'. But we understood, for once in a while a man had to feel what was known as 'peart' when the cares of stock were clouded by the juice of the Black Taunton apple.

My first year on the land was a varied life: an anthology, where every chapter had its particular charm, whether it was pulling charlock among the peas, driving the four-horse team among the cattle and sheep, climbing the thirty-rung ladders for the fruit, going out with the gun or picking the frozen sprouts with the men. Though I'm sure there were easier ways of earning twelve shillings a week.

I can picture now my hide under the wall in what was called a cave, with the gun, sitting on a hamper with my dinner of bread and home cured bacon, a bottle of luke warm tea, a packet of Woodbines, watching the February larks rise and twitter high above, the crows building their nests in the elms. The blue and white of the hungry wood pigeons rising in clouds from the sprout tops, then later watching the mad March hares box and gambol on Furse Hill. Sampling the first strawberries, the early hay plums in July, young peas, new potatoes and the glow of the fireside on returning from the sting of an east wind. What else could a boy wish for. Then the Saturday nights at the Scala, the silent screen. Worry, nerves – I only knew them as words.

The sweetness of life was from field and hedgerow and hill, the benefit of a rabbit dinner, of apple dumplings, the home-cured bacon from the cottage pig. Money was something talked about by the town folk. It never bought the peace, the comradeship of a 1920 village. As the blind gypsy said, 'The sun, the moon, the stars, the wind on the heath. Life is sweet, brother.'

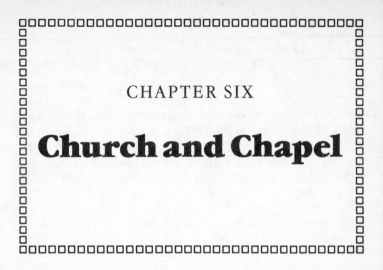

CHAPTER SIX

Church and Chapel

Our parish church, the only one in England dedicated to Saint Barbara until the 'thirties, when I gather another one had her as its patron saint, was a far cry from Chapel. St Barbara is the patron saint of builders. The legend about her is quite unique. When she became a Christian she was locked in a tower by her jealous father, she was so beautiful. She is also the patron saint of gunsmiths and gunpowder. The stokehole in Italian men-of-war is known as the Santa Barbara. In times of thunder and lightning St Barbara has been called on or invoked. The stained glass window in the church, a gift of a member of the Baldwyn family, shows St Barbara with three towers, Father, Son and Holy Ghost.

The church was dedicated to St Barbara because it once belonged to the monks of Barbe-en-Ange in Normandy. The earliest portion of the present building is the south wall of the nave, two-foot-nine-inch-thick masonry of the Norman period. As time went on the church gradually became enlarged by the addition of a fourteen-century chantry at the north-east corner of the nave, lengthened to form an aisle. In 1624 a new chancel on Gothic lines replaced the Norman one. The porch, originally fourteenth century, has a little door alongside it which the squire entered, the Baldwyn family who occupied the squire's pew.

It's unusual that St Barbara lies at the bottom end of the village, but the moat pond nearby was the monk's fish pond and a ditch and mound above show the remains of an earlier moated house. One can imagine how important the moat pond was in ancient times for fishing, north Gloucestershire being so far from the sea.

The entrance to the churchyard has a row of drooping ash trees which were planted there by my grandfather, William Archer, for Squire William Henry Baldwyn about 1850. They lead to a copper beech tree which has grown so tall it dwarfs a struggling yew tree. The giant yew tree which stands in the middle of the old churchyard is hundreds of years old. Some say yews were planted to provide bows to shoot arrows while it's more likely the tree was a fertility symbol. The yews and the copper beech give a sense of time and eternity to the place, and drooping ashes seem to ape the gargoyles of the bell tower. They cross and knot their branches in a peculiar fashion, untamed trees, wild and grim. The lychgate at the entrance, built in 1928, was a mistake; it obscures the view of church and graveyard. The fifteenth century cross stands before it.

I only went to church with Dad at harvest festivals, the rest of the time we went to Chapel; I found religion there less personal, and didn't agree with some of the creed, but psalm singing was quite beautiful if the vicar had a good voice to lead; Church had its own form of exclusivity. The hymn-singing didn't have the enthusiasm of Chapel, each hymn ending with A-r-men, while Aymen was the rule at Chapel. There were rules about the colour of the flower arrangements. Never red flowers on Good Friday. Lent was a time to deny oneself of sugar or something. Confirmation was instead of Conversion, infant Baptism a must before Confirmation. Holy Communion in the morning to remember the Last Supper seemed odd and no food to be had before that sacrament. The church organ was quite grand compared with the Chapel harmonium. It must have been better still there when the village orchestra played in the old gallery, a remnant of the old minstrels.

Rev. Margetts was what's known as a low churchman, so he did work with the Chapel folk, visiting all and sundry in illness or bereavement.

Chapel was a constant thorn in the flesh of a young boy. There was often a blight from that little pulpit, a condemnation, quite

Children at the cross

unnecessary, which really did no more than boost the ego of some local preacher. The remnant of Victorian Puritanism was still as wounding as ever. It created a distinct line, or tried to create a line, between the Saved and the Damned.

Preachers varied at Chapel like chalk and cheese. The compassionate man who maybe cycled miles to preach the Gospel, The Good News; the Holier Than Thou, miserable men who poured out their message of the lake of fire until the smell of brimstone drowned the smell of the worshippers.

Sankey's sacred songs and solos with their rousing choruses were so often dimmed by the address. Some of the words puzzled and perplexed a boy of ten.

> Blessed be the fountain of blood
> to a world of sinners revealed.
> Blessed be the dear Son of God,
> Only by His stripes are we healed.

Then a chorus,

Are you washed?

The answer,

Yes, I'm washed in the blood, in the soul cleansing blood of the lamb.

Are your garments spotless, are they white as snow, are you washed in the blood of the lamb?

The thought of human blood sickened me, as one doggerel after another spelt out, not a human love affair with the Almighty with an uplifting spirit, but a kind of superstitious Baptism of blood.

The ideas of redemption did more than anything to make me refuse to take part in Holy Communion, for the original idea of observing The Last Supper had been twisted into a bogus exclusive ceremony. Years later, reading C.S. Lewis's book, *Your God is Too Small*, I was convinced how insular the worship of the Almighty had become. The Druids worshipped the sun, a light more realistic than a blood bath.

I liked the tunes of the service, but not the words. The vision of a life in hell, in torment, in the lake of fire was frightening, for so many believed it to be the doom of what were known as the unconverted. Missionaries were the bane of my life: dark-suited gentlemen who came with the threat of destruction, except for the Chosen Few. After the address when all the demons of hell were vividly described, the appeal went out for converts. To ignore the appeal appeared to me an end of life like Fred Randalls's cows on the fire. But worse than that, the fire never went out.

Then came the after meeting. 'All who must go, please leave quietly,' during the final silent prayer. All heads bowed in silent prayer and it took courage to make for the door as the squeaking boots of the missionary passed the pew on his way to do his buttonholing. 'Good night. Have you taken Christ as your Saviour?' These words as I escaped through the door to the starlight outside cut at the heart like a knife: unChrist-like, unChristian.

The after meeting would go on another hour if I stayed. Men and women would get to their feet, giving their testimony – a description of their life of sin before conversion. It was a dreadful experience. Some preachers emphasized that it was not enough to believe in the heart, but one was not saved until a Witness was made openly in front of everyone. The whole congregation sang dirge-like hymns. The preacher prayed that those unsaved who had left would be under conviction of sin and would never sleep until they yielded to Christ. How I longed for an experience when the load of sin piled on me by these folk, and by no one else, could be lifted, not by the force of threats of hell, but by the love of the Almighty.

I was thankful that Dad would come out with me and escape the after meeting, while the rest of the family stayed behind. He never said much about the life of the spirit, neither did he stay to Communion, or The Lord's Supper.

Sometimes the preacher, maybe an uneducated man, had a kind message to deliver: these men I believe were the salt of the earth, a race which has gone.

The first Sunday in every month, Mr William Boulton took the service. What a good man he was. He was just bubbling over with compassion and spoke of the Better Land. His words were full of promise and joy.

There was, however, a lighter side to those frightful Sunday nights; there was entertainment of a sort when Pastor Penrose came and sang to his banjo accompaniment 'Feasting With My Lord'.

Mr Rickings was a star turn if you could put up with his tears as he threw himself into his hot gospelling. He did throw himself physically one memorable night after the collection. The basket of coppers and a little silver was near the pulpit on the platform. Mr Rickings stampeded backwards and forwards with the two pictures of Eternal Bliss for the converted and the Lake of Fire for the unbeliever. He caught his foot and stumbled, pent-up with emotion. His other foot kicked the collection basket off the platform. It bowled up the aisle past me as he cried, 'Filthy lucre.' Our collection lay on the red carpet in a little stream of silver and bronze.

How pure the air was away from the wintergreen, the eucalyptus, the camphor balls, the organist's Soir de Paris, away from the frightening hallelujahs, the amens, the response of yes and no, when the words were digested by some of the hard core of Puritanism.

When Mr George Cave, retired curator of the botanical gardens in Darjeeling, wore them, spats spread through the Chapel folk like an epidemic. Mr Cave and Mr George Hughes the artist both wore spats. Soon the young local preachers of the Chapel could be seen on Sundays in spats, with their navy blue suits, and two or three ventured out in bowler hats and had little crêpe de chine handkerchiefs peeping from their breast pockets. This, with the scent of Jockey Club brilliantine, to me added nothing to their pulpit performances. Shepherd Tidmarsh remarked wistfully one Sunday as he met me in the road after the preacher had passed by, 'What sights you see when you haven't got your gun.'

Older preachers stuck to the Victorian type broad cloth suits with four buttons and wore the pure white Come to Jesus (starched) shirt fronts, red spotted handkerchiefs mopped their brows when the sermon was almost spent. Dad wore a good fawn tweed suit on Sundays and a soft velour type trilby hat with a deep furrow from back to front.

The secretary announced at Chapel on Sunday night, 'Now, next Wednesday, we are to be favoured with an organ recital by Miss Baldwyn.' Then with a broad smile, 'Miss Burrage is coming over from Evesham to sing a few solos. Well, to break the monotony of the music. Now on Saturday it's our annual Sunday School Tay. You are all invited, the koyr, the congregation and anyone who has ever shown an interest in this place. The tay will start at approximately about half past five I should think. But will the ladies,' broad smile, 'get there early for you know what it says in the Word, "The night cometh when no man can walk".'

In the Recreation Room these annual events were the highlight of the religious year, for after tea the games, organized by William Boulton, varied from musical chairs, clap and run, a-hunting we will go, to a tug-of-war with a waggon rope, all under the paraffin lamps. I remember Sir Roger De Coverley was allowed, but no dancing, for dancing was considered sinful.

However, after some of the older folk had left, someone would say, 'Let's have a gig around.' The piano played the tunes for foxtrots and quicksteps, and it was rumoured that when the washing up was done from the copper boiler, two of the ladies who had organized the tea used the hot water for an annual bath in a galvanized bath in the back room behind the billiard table. The dust from the floorboards and the heat from the red hot stove sometimes started what was known as, 'Something that's going round' in the village, which varied from sore throats to flu.

The Recreation Room was fully used in winter, replacing the old Reading Room where, in a confined space above a stable, some young folk had learnt to play the violin from a Miss Millward. Lantern lectures on Sunday nights after Chapel with a carbide lantern operated by Mr Wigley were somewhere to go. The British and Foreign Bible Society organized these. Sometimes a missionary came from a place like Java and showed black-and-white slides of giraffe-necked women with their peculiar collars, topless but with straw skirts. Frank and I tittered from our seat by the stove. The meeting always began by us singing, 'The Church's One Foundation'. That was to please both Church and Chapel folk. Once the lantern caught fire and we made a hasty exit while Mr Wigley with flaming acetylene gas coped with the flames.

CHAPTER SEVEN

The Outside World

BLUE DISTANCES

It's often been said that views from Bredon Hill are blue distances. The pure clear air on the summit acts as a giant telescope to the Vale below and the Cotswold Edge and Malvern. The colours change from the pale green of the Malverns where the turf is like a close clipped carpet to the distant blue of Meon Hill way towards Stratford. Our world was small. We were Gloucestershire and so proud of it, yet hemmed in by Worcestershire on three sides.

Sunday afternoon walks with Grandad were excursions into Worcestershire, to Kersoe and Elmley Castle. By a brook bridge at the foot of Furze Hill the road surface changed from the yellow stone quarried on Bredon to a blue surface, maybe stone from faraway Clee Hill. The world was a square of land under the hill, on the eastern side bounded by Kersoe, Worcestershire, Sedgeberrow.

I went to Worcestershire with Dad on the horse dray with loads of oats to be ground into flour at Sedgeberrow Mill on the River Isbourne (Conderton to the South West). Locals said, ' 'Tis the only little river in England to flow north.' What a fable – it suited me to believe it. To see the great wheel turn as the sluices let the water down from the mill pond and listen to the giant cogs turn the millstones as the building vibrated was a music, a presence of the past.

The miller, coated like a powdered lady in flour, was a little man with an enormous nose. 'Don't you say anything about the Miller's nose,' Dad warned me as we went gently down Sedgeberrow Bank with Tom the nag in the dray. It seemed that I as a boy of about four couldn't resist the miller's nose. 'Look Daddy, that man's nose.' With a well deserved box of my ears I said no more, but marvelled at the water machinery. When we took ten sacks of oats to the mill we always took with us one or two spare empty sacks. A sack of oats produces a little more than a sack of flour, I learnt. And didn't the miller's horse always look the best fed, but Dad said it was the scrapings from the millstones which fed him so well.

We didn't take any wheat to be ground, for the sack which had stood in the pantry during the submarine scare was still half full. A little before my first journey to the mill was the last raid of the German zeppelins when PC Smith came late at night and said the zeppelins were coming over. The curtains which blacked out the bedroom were dark red velvet but before the curtains went up that night all the candles were blown out and Dad struggled in the dark while we all sat on the big bed in Grandad's room. I reckon Grandad Westwood was an early pacifist, but he never said so. He would never kill anything, yet he loved fishing in his boat on moonlight nights on the River Avon. There was peace away from Grandma who was always in command.

The zeppelins bombed Tipton station that morning, so I heard the family say, and the blast from a bomb threw Uncle Bill out of a coal truck, but Constable Fred Smith was doing his duty by warning us. He was a regular visitor to our house as he lived in one of our cottages. When he put the handcuffs on me one evening by the fire and my little hands slipped out of them, Grandad laughed and Grandma looked a bit stern. 'Handcuffs are for criminals,' she said, but the men in blue were my friends. It gave me a sense of being safe that PC Smith lived across the road.

One thing worried me, an old railway carriage in his garden. It was painted black and it was said that this old carriage was the policeman's prison where he kept bad boys all night. His garden backed onto the churchyard. No one ever ran up the churchyard path, but silently, reverently, walked past the gravestones. I always ran past the copper beech tree as far as the churchyard yew until the railway carriage was out of sight. When Grandad told me, 'It's only Mr Smith's fowl run,' a great weight fell from my mind, knowing that PC Smith didn't lock naughty boys up in his garden and feed them on bread and water like some boys said.

The zeppelins never came again but bombed the Black Country that night, taking their sights from the blast furnaces of Tipton and Oldbury. I thought it very funny when Uncle Bill came by train one weekend and told us how the blast had thrown him from a railway truck. Mother always said Uncle Bill was coarse when he spent his evenings in the Plough and Harrow drinking cider and told me, 'Drink cider and make your belly wider.' 'Belly' was a disgusting word in front of Mother. The word 'liar' was also banned. 'Stomach' and 'stories' were more refined than 'belly' and 'lies'.

About ten miles away from the village near the banks of the Severn river is a little village called Ripple. Here Auntie Phoebe lived with Uncle Jack. One Sunday Dad put Polly the mare into the governess car and we were to go and see Auntie Phoebe for tea. She was much older than Dad, in fact she had a daughter who was older than him. It was early in May when the apple blossom coloured every orchard around Pershore. I saw for the first time the other side of Bredon Hill and the vast expanse of Defford Common alive with scraggy sheep and their lambs. It looked a backwater, with unkempt sheep, uncared for. Every hawthorn bush and gorse had combed part of the fleeces of these ragged animals. We reached Upton-on-Severn, calling at a salt-glazed horse trough in the little town for Polly to have a drink.

Auntie Phoebe greeted Dad like a Mother greets a son. 'Well Tom how be ya?' she said throwing her great arms around him. Then she kissed us all, and how I hated that. Never had I seen such a woman. Over twenty stone in weight, dressed in a black shiny silk-like dress which she overflowed. Uncle Jim said that when Phoebe travelled by train she rode in the guard's van for if she got into a railway carriage she had great difficulty in getting out again.

The table was laid for Sunday tea: home-baked bread, farm butter, jams of all descriptions and a big currant cake. The cottage was a little museum of the farm labourers of long ago. A what-not loaded with china, gilded mirrors, a long sofa, a sofa table, the black iron kettle sang on the hob.

Uncle Jack was a cowman. A little squat man in breeches and gaiters, his face was almost covered with greying hair and in between the whiskers, red patches of weatherbeaten, sun-scorched skin made a picture roughly framed with his beard, moustache and side-whiskers. He looked a cross between an inn-keeper and a groom with his red spotted waistcoat, no doubt put on for Mother and Dad's benefit that Sunday.

We paraded the village, after tying Polly the mare up to a post on the village green where the stocks still stood, menacing, waiting for some sheep stealer off Defford Common to be pinioned there and take the insults of the just. Auntie Phoebe walked with a stick, breathless, and took us into the little church. I looked for Uncle Jack but when we returned he was sitting on a pig bench by his pig sty drinking a mug of cider.

At the tea table my eyes wandered around the sitting room where nearly all the flowered wallpaper was covered with old photographs. Uncles, aunts, great uncles, great aunts, old William Archer with his donkey and cart. Farley Archer his cousin loading his wagon of hay on his smallholding at Enfield Cottage.

We drove home on that evening in late Spring and for once missed going to Chapel, but Dad said Phoebe was middling, very middling, and he thought he should visit her. We never went again, but a black edged envelope from Uncle Jack told us the news that she had 'Passed Away'.

A little while after seeing the German prisoners of war working the land at Sanfield Farm and marching to their billets up Sedgeberrow Hill, Armistice was declared.

Cousin Tom had always called when he was on leave. He fought in France in the Worcestershire Regiment. He looked so smart in his uniform and I used to ask him to unroll the puttees from his legs and show me how he put them on. Mother made a fuss of him and bought him Gold Flake cigarettes every time he came. Tom joined the Forces earlier than he need have done but a woman who lived up the Hill Lane used to give him a white feather every Sunday after Chapel, and he was just seventeen years old. His elder brother Charlie was killed early one morning in Mesopotamia by a sniper's bullet as he was brewing tea on the edge of the trenches. Another young man who had worked for

Dad overstayed his leave on getting married, suffered field punishment in France, being tied to a gun carriage wheel. The Germans advanced, the Worcesters retreated, and young John was filled with lead.

Two Conchies worked on our farm living in a caravan. They were very quiet lads and took the insults of the women's Sunday presents of white feathers after Chapel without a murmur. But some folk said, 'They dodged the column,' whatever that meant.

After the Armistice, the men who returned to our village walked past our house from the station. When we knew anyone who was due from the train, my brother and I waved Union Jack flags from the window of the living room. All these men had a welcome, but the one I remember most of all was Charlie Lippet of the Royal Army Veterinary Corps. He was a sergeant, a farrier sergeant, the smartest man I ever saw. Charlie wore spurs around his ankles and marched alone past our house as if on the parade ground: a fearless man with horses who later worked on the land handling half-broken colts like kittens.

Charlie was one of a big family and his mother did some of our washing, bringing it down on Saturday afternoons from her cottage with all the news of the week. Her husband, known as Tat, lost an eye hedge cropping and the glass one didn't quite match. 'How's your husband?' Mother would say. 'Oh Mam, he's got that bronchitical cataract again you know.' When her spaniel dog came in the house he used to cock his leg against the door, but no one seemed to mind.

The summer after the Armistice the Peace Celebrations were held in The Little Piece field. After dark a bonfire was lit by Doctor Roberson. He was at that time a great man in our village. The good old Doctor served on the Medical Board, vetting men for the forces. Cousin Tom's brother George went before him. He had bad feet, hammer toes. The Doctor said, 'Leave him be on the land, he'll do a better job behind the plough.' Another member of the board asked him how he walked behind the plough and George said, 'Oh, I hang on to the implement.'

After the bonfire had been lit Captain Ewart Morrison, that film-star like officer, lit the fireworks. The rockets soared above the Wynch Field, some cases dropped in The Little Piece. I was shepherded around the field by Dad and Mr Sandford, and Mr Sandford collected the rocket cases for me to keep as a memento.

By the light of the fire Dr Roberson threw pennies high in the air to be scrambled for by the village boys. Tom Hunting my cousin was there and told us how Mrs Roberson the doctor's wife sent cigarettes and chocolates regularly to the Ashton boys at the front.

The following evening all the ex-Servicemen were treated to a supper at the school. Standing with Grandad Westwood I watched them go in, their new ribbons and medals, pinned on their jacket lapels. One man who had served in the Balkans had a string of ribbons and medals which swung from him like a martingale horse brass.

THE PEACE CELEBRATION

It was late when the sound of 'Land of Hope and Glory' sung with such gusto ended the display. Mr Sandford, a gardener from Close Cottage, with a carbide cycle lamp, led my brother and me around the dying fire and we searched for the rocket cases to take home just to remember the special occasion.

As we walked home along Blacksmiths Lane Dad pointed out to me for the very first time Jack and his Waggon, the pattern of stars correctly known as the Plough and the Pole star, north of the village. The stars represented the horses pulling the waggon and seemed so near, yet so far away. I'd never been out on a starlit night before and likened Jack and his Waggon to Ralph the carter with the team in the hayfield. It impressed me more than the fireworks, for Jack and his Waggon didn't fall from the sky like the rockets had done. They stayed, and Dad said they would always be there in the northern sky, eternal as the sun and the moon.

MARKET

In the old market at Gloucester the square was filled on Saturdays with country men in breeches. Some wore bowler hats, others pork pie trilbies, while the farm workers and the drovers wore caps and corduroy trousers. Nearly everyone carried a stick: varying from the long thumb stick to the bamboo cane sticks of the dealers. Mr Pope, one auctioneer, wore a grey bowler, breeches, cloth gaiters and a yellow waistcoat. He always had a flower in the buttonhole of the lapel of his jacket, usually a carnation.

Dad bought calves almost every Saturday. As each of our cows calved we bought two more to suckle with her own and then every three months a bunch of calves were weaned from the cows and replacement calves under a week old bought at market. Every cross-bred Hereford calf which Dad bid for was first tested as a potential beef animal by placing the four fingers of the hand between its shoulder blade bones. A calf with that width between its bones would make a good beast.

Education was a drudge at grammar school, but I learned more listening to Mr Norman Bruton at the auctioneer's rostrum among the din of bawling cows and calves and the 'Mind your backs' call of the man who drove them to the sale ring; more of life and of people, and watched the little man and his wife milk the cows by hand. What pluck these couple of milkers had as they sat on three-legged stools and milked strange cows, kicking cows upset from the peace of the farms they came from.

We took the old two hundredweight and a quarter corn sacks to market and Dad and I slipped the calves into them like sleeping bags and tied the sacks around the top and, with the back seat removed from the car, loaded maybe four calves ready for home. This was common practice and they travelled more comfortably than in some draughty cattle truck. Cattle lorries were rare.

In my new outfit I watched the cheap jacks such as the herbalist with a spirit stove and kettle dishing out glasses of herb tea to farriers, and selling the herbs; a man with a constant stream of patter of politics and religion cut a piece of leather into leather laces, his sharp knife slid through the leather on his table like a hot knife through butter. He cut them in pairs, leaving an uncut piece at one end. I believe they were fourpence [2p] a pair, so we were never short of leather laces.

Our midday meal was at the Wessex Temperance Hotel; Dad being teetotal, we rarely went to the Spread Eagle. A tight-lipped, tall, thin lady read the menu. There was really no need; it never varied. Steak and kidney pudding, roast beef, roast pork, boiled mutton, apple tart, plum tart, rice pudding. Dad usually had the beef and rarely ate pork as he always said he was a martyr to indigestion, and took herb tea for that. The smell of the steak and kidney pudding, steaming hot, took my fancy; the puddings were bigger than cricket balls and full of meat.

Ginger, one of the many hangers on at the Market, had helped us bag the calves. A down-trodden specimen of humanity, unshaven and ragged. He always asked for the price of a cup of tea, but I watched him take the money to the Spread Eagle for something stronger. The drovers in brown smocks plastered with raddle from marking the sheep and carrying scissors to mark the cows for the dealers by clipping strange patterns on their rumps, marks known only to them, were a sight to remember. Cattle were parted in the pens into groups. The drovers, using their sticks in a deft manner, made an aisle between them like the parting of the water of the Red Sea.

The markets of Evesham, Tewkesbury and Gloucester were a mixture on what Dad called 'fair days' of farm workers, farmers and the town people, known as outrights or outriders, now called reps. These men were smartly suited, a race apart, and carried samples of seeds and fertilizer. One Mr Phillips was immaculate. He sold fertilizer, but was very deaf.

'You'll have five tons of hoof and horn Tom,' he'd say to Dad.

'No, THREE tons, Mr Phillips,' Dad would reply, and before this professional merchant had cupped his ear to listen, he'd put five tons in his order book. One farmer neighbour of ours, a bit of a wag, said that one had to shout sulphate of ammonia in one of his partly deaf ears, and superphosphate in the other.

Every spring the round of travellers came to the farm, some selling, some begging. Outrights came with samples of seed and artificial manure. Hurdy gurdies played in the village lane causing the dogs to howl and bark.

Everything that was turned by wheels fascinated me. Scissor grinders made blue sparks fly from their grinding wheels. Some came with wheel carts and parked by the village cross and pedalled: the magic of gears, the power of the pedals, were wonders in a little world where the five-mile drive to Evesham was to another country.

The packman came loaded with suit and dress material, boots and shoes. Dad bought enough cloth to make a suit for me. He bought two pairs of lace-up black boots, my first pair, a promotion from the strapped shoes. A miniature pair like Dad's Sunday boots. Little Dukes they were called, while my big brother Tom had Little Gents.

SUN, MOON AND STARS

When bedtime came in our oil-lamp and candle-lit farmhouse, I slept under the sloping eaves in an iron bedstead with shining brass knobs at the bed ends. The candles' flicker created a little world of shadows on the flowered wallpaper. The brass knobs shone like two little stars at the foot of the bed. I was afraid of the dark and snuggled deep down under the counterpane-covered bedclothes and the tick featherbed underneath formed a nest-like haven to dream on. The big golden moon gleaming through the dormers was a comfort.

All was silent until the rats did their circus act in the hollow walls between the wattle and daub and the plaster wall. They thundered round squeaking and squealing on cold winter's nights after they had taken shelter from the bleak icy stubbles and grass fields. The rats became an accepted night time feature of life in an old half-timbered house which had stood for three hundred years near the church and the crossroads.

Old men told tales of how the calendar was studied and parties were planned at the full moon. I was curious about the heavenly spectacle as I walked the hill with Dad or the village street. The story of the creation was explained in a very primitive way, but it satisfied curiosity. Dad called the Plough, Jack and his Waggon, and the two stars at the back of the waggon-shaped stencil of the sky pointed to the Pole star. The village street ran due north and south so on clear nights the Pole star pointed the way to Elmley Castle.

The year was 1927 and I believe the month was June when we were told at school that a total eclipse of the sun was due early one morning and that it would never be seen in Britain again until either 2000 or 2001. Would I be still here, I wondered, for I would be in my eighties by then. We just could not afford to miss this phenomenon and a great trek was organized to be at the Cuckoo Pen on Little Hill early that morning at four o'clock.

It was a usual dawn setting by the great oak trees in Church Close when a few of us climbed the hill towards the Cuckoo Pen, that clump of beech trees on a plateau which formed a ten-acre amphitheatre on the approach to the steep climb to the summit. The rooks, already awake, cawed from the nests in the tall elms alongside the Close orchards, nests vacated by their young on the May 12th. Peewits were noisy on the ground and the young rabbits scuttled to their burrows near the ash tree where they had a big earth, an earth which had been their home since time immemorial. The grass was soaking with dew as the dimness before the dawn gave a companionable eeriness to the scene.

At the Cuckoo Pen Mr Cave was already there with a piece of smoked glass to view the spectacle of the sun's imminent complete obliteration by the moon. My brother and John Cave and I had smoked over a fire pieces of broken lemonade bottles, a kind of inverted telescope to look through. 'Don't look directly at the sun when it rises, that can damage your eyes.' Mr Cave, the retired curator of Darjeeling's botanical gardens, knew more about the natural things of plants, birds and nature in general than any of us green hobbledehoys of the village.

A golden streak of light shone like a thread of tapestry along the whole sky line of the Cotswold Edge. We waited. By now the whole world of nature was awake. The full-grown rabbits had gone to ground, leaving their young to be daring enough to crop the burrow-side grass. The holts or burrows thumped underfoot as the parent animals warned their young of our approach.

Gradually the scene of sunrise took its eternal pattern as the long golden dawn grew wider minute by minute. Nothing unusual, just a sight which we had seen enacted so often on the edge of day. A crescent of the sun peeped over the horizon like the slender arch of a bridge. Growing minute by minute until half of the golden ball, the colour of a blood orange, lit the hill, but behind the trees the shadows of silhouette copper of the beeches lay on the glistening dew-drenched hill, long and beautiful like fallen trees. I put my smoked glass viewfinder to my eyes and watched the sun until the whole globe of gold stood like a solid waggon wheel on Broadway Hill.

Directly above, the full moon lay like silver in the sky. The two great lamps of our earth were apparently getting closer together until the moon blacked out a rind of its powerful ray. No one spoke. The quietness could be felt. Perhaps it was Mr Cave's lifelong experience of the outdoor world which dictated in silence the need for us to watch and wait.

Two cuckoos answered each other from the oak trees below. The rooks were noisy, toing and froing from elm to elm. Soon the silvery moon had covered half the sun. It seemed to creep in front of Phoebus like a blind half-drawn over a window. By now the Cuckoo Pen with that little group of villagers had their smoked glass screens over their eyes towards the eastern sky as the sun was screened until only a crescent of light illuminated the dawn. We waited.

It almost seemed that the birds knew what was happening, or were they surprised at this quite peculiar dawn? They became quiet and fled to their night-time perches in trees and hedgerow. The noisy blackbirds stilled their song, then came a darkness as dark and inky as the darkest night, so complete, so absolute, that I lost sight of my brother Tom, John and Mr Cave. It was night again as for once in a lifetime Nature had been fooled. I wondered what primitive men had thought, as they must have witnessed such a spectacle long before astronomy had explained it. Science

213

has taught us that this is only temporary, that daylight reappears as sure as day follows night. No need for smoked glasses for an instant which seemed an age.

At last a crescent of golden light no wider than a straw of wheat gleamed from behind the moon. With glass up to my eyes I saw it grow like a second sunrise. The shadows of the beeches returned. A cock crowed in the Vale below. When half the waggon wheel of sunlight returned the birds came from their nightly perches and sang again. From the Church Close oaks, cuckoo, cuckoo, rang as a signal that normality, a normality which had deserted us momentarily, had returned.

When the whole golden ball of sunshine gave daylight that June morning, silently we pocketed our smoked glass to keep as a memento of the occasion. Mr Cave laughed a quiet, jolly laugh. Maybe he had seen such a spectacle before abroad, but he told us he'd never see another, for the year 2000 was a long way off for one of Nature's gentlemen, a man honoured by the King for his research, his contribution to the exploration of the mysteries of the Himalayas. 'Summer and winter, seedtime and harvest shall not cease as long as the earth remaineth,' he said with all the faith and trust in the God he loved.

James Herriot
Vets Might Fly £1.95

A severe case of World War Two takes James Herriot away from his vet's life in the Dales and into a training camp somewhere in England . . .

'There are funny cases, sad cases, farm animals and pets, downright dialect-speaking farmers, ladies of retirement, hard-bitten NCOs and of course the immortal Siegfried and Tristan' SUNDAY TIMES

Let Sleeping Vets Lie £1.95

The hilarious revelations of James Herriot, the now famous vet in the Yorkshire Dales, continue his happy story of everyday tribulations with unwilling animal patients and their richly diverse owners.

'He can tell a good story against himself, and his pleasure in the beauty of the countryside in which he works is infectious' DAILY TELEGRAPH

Vets in Harness £1.95

With the fourth of this superb series, James Herriot again takes us on his varied and often hair-raising journeys to still more joyous adventures in the Yorkshire Dales.

'Animal magic . . . James Herriot provokes a chuckle or a lump in your throat in every chapter' DAILY MIRROR

James Herriot
If Only They Could Talk £1.95

The genial misadventures of James Herriot, a young vet in the lovely
Yorkshire Dales are enough to make a cat laugh – let alone the animals, if only
they could talk.

Vet in a Spin £1.95

Strapped into the cockpit of a Tiger Moth trainer, James Herriot has swapped
his wellingtons and breeches for sheep-skin boots and a baggy flying suit. But
the vet-turned-airman is the sort of trainee to terrify flying instructors who've
faced the Luftwaffe without flinching. Very soon he's grounded, discharged
and back to his old life in the dales around Darrowby.

'Marks the emergence of Herriot as a mature writer' YORKSHIRE POST

'Just as much fun as its predecessors. May it sell, as usual, in its millions!'
THE TIMES

The Lord God Made Them All £2.95

The war is over, the RAF uniform has been handed in and James Herriot goes
back to where he ought to be – at work in the dales around Darrowby. Much
has changed, but the blunt-spoken Yorkshire folk and the host of four-legged
patients are still the same. So is their vet, not knowing that literary success is
just around the corner.

'A joyous book, a celebration of life itself' PUBLISHERS WEEKLY

John Holgate
Make a Cow Laugh £1.75

To give up commuter life for the daily grind of a Welsh border farm takes something special. You might need imagination, dedication or just sheer lunacy . . . but you do need a sense of humour!

'Packed with humorous incidents . . . if his farming is as good as his writing he should have left London years ago' WESTERN MAIL

Tom Sharpe
Indecent Exposure £1.95

The brilliant follow-up to *Riotous Assembly* . . . another of Tom Sharpe's hilarious and savage satires on South Africa . . .

'Explosively funny, fiendishly inventive' SUNDAY TIMES

'A lusty and delightfully lunatic fantasy' SUNDAY EXPRESS

Riotous Assembly £1.95

A crime of passion committed with a multi-barrelled elephant gun . . . A drunken bishop attacked by a pack of Alsatians in a swimming pool . . . Transvestite variations in a distinguished lady's rubber-furnished bedroom . . . Famous battles re-enacted by five hundred schizophrenic Zulus and an equal number of (equally mad) whites . . .

'Crackling, spitting, murderously funny' DAILY TELEGRAPH

Tom Sharpe
Porterhouse Blue £1.95

To Porterhouse College, Cambridge, famous for rowing, low academic
standards and a proud cuisine, comes a new Master, an ex-grammar school
boy, demanding Firsts, women students, a self-service canteen and a
slot-machine for contraceptives, to challenge the established order – with
catastrophic results . . .

'That rarest and most joyous of products – a highly intelligent funny book'
SUNDAY TIMES

The Great Pursuit £1.95

The hilarious new bestseller from the author of *Wilt*.

'Frensic . . . a snuff-taking, port-drinking literary agent . . . receives a
manuscript from an anonymous author's solicitor – "an odyssey of lust . . . a
filthy story with an even filthier style." Foreseeing huge profits in the US,
Frensic places the book with the Al Capone of American publishing,
Hutchmeyer, "the most illiterate publisher in the world" . . .' LISTENER

'The funniest novelist writing today' THE TIMES

Blott on the Landscape £1.95

'Skulduggery at stately homes, dirty work at the planning inquiry, and the
villains falling satisfactorily up to their ears in the minestrone . . . the heroine
breakfasts on broken bottles, wears barbed wire next to her skin and stops at
nothing to protect her ancestral seat from a motorway construction'
THE TIMES

'Deliciously English comedy' GUARDIAN

Peter Tinniswood
The Brigadier Down Under £1.75

In the not inconsequential tradition of *Tales From a Long Room* and
More Tales from a Long Room.

'Esteemed reader, far, far the mountain peak, as one of our English poets
essayed, yet not as far as the distant landscapes of Australia from the familiar
surroundings of my own beloved Witney Scrotum . . . I could not but follow
our own fine team to their Herculean test of leather and willow on the
far-flung turf . . . Australia is a land disturbingly full of Australians . . . Not a
place to which I took an instant affection. The lady wife was more adaptable,
especially in terms of her powers of rainmaking and skill in the nets . . . I am
not a prejudiced man, but . . .'

The Brigadier in Season £1.75

It's the start of another cricket season and spring is coursing its way
rampantly through the Brigadier's veins. Having finally abandoned all hope of
being selected to open the batting for England, he settles down to
reminiscence. With charm and candour, speaking from the depths of his
deckchair at the Witney Scrotum cricket ground, he passes with pungent wit
over such subjects as the day they discovered that the Commodore's
gardener was none other than Hermann Goering, and many others
guaranteed to entertain.

The Brigadier's Brief Lives £1.75

Now safely re-ensconced in his beloved Witney Scrotum after a somewhat
hazardous trip down under, the true blue, indefatigable brigadier is once more
pontificating long and loud. We now see his outrageously prejudiced
judgements being inflicted upon certain persons in the public eye – the
famous, the not-so-famous, cricketers, journalists, even royalty. These
scurrilous portraits are as rampantly bigoted, muddled and inaccurate as ever.

George MacDonald Fraser
Royal Flash £1.95

The second part of the now celebrated Flashman Papers – that saga of triumphant dishonour – reveals how Sir Harry Flashman VC, the arch cad and lecher, confuses the Schleswig-Holstein question. Lured to Germany by an unscrupulous adventuress, Flash Harry is soon involved in a desperate succession of escapes, disguises and amours.

The General Danced at Dawn £1.50

Fall in for laughter with Private McAuslan, the dirtiest soldier in the world. Proceed to Brigade Highland Games via the regimental football team tour of the Med, troop train from Cairo to Jerusalem, a general court-martial and guard mounting at Edinburgh Castle . . .

'Hilarious episodes in the Service life on and off duty of a young officer and the men he commanded – rough, tough but lovable Jocks'
ABERDEEN PRESS and JOURNAL

Mr American £2.50

When Mark J. Franklin stepped ashore from the *Mauretania* in Liverpool in 1909, his luggage included a pair of Remington .44s, a Mexican saddle and a fortune courtesy of a silver mine in Tonopah, Nebraska. Tall, rich and handsome, he soon found that money talked in Edwardian England. From Shaftesbury Avenue to Sandringham he cut a dash through society, and married the ravishing jewel of the county set. The mysterious Mr American – a man with a shadowy past and some very sinister enemies . . .

'Every page is sheer pleasure' THE TIMES

'The sort of book that can keep you armchair-locked all day' NOW!

George MacDonald Fraser
McAuslan in the Rough £1.50

That walking disaster Private McAuslan, the dirtiest soldier in the world, is back for more misadventures – from the bars of North Africa to the fast greens of Scotland.

'A delight with a chuckle on every page' DAILY MIRROR

'An old sweats' reunion, the nearest we could hope to get to a neo-Kipling touch' GUARDIAN

The Pyrates £2.50

What have we here? Out yonder on the high seas of adventure are Pyrates! Can our impossibly handsome hero redeem the treasure and rescue his lovely lady from the lascivious clutches of Akbar the Damned? Read on, and all shall be revealed.

'It's all there, right down to a dead man's chest, cleavages that are everything they should be and characters in seaboots who say nothing but 'Arr' or 'Me, Hearty!' THE FINANCIAL TIMES

Flashman £2.50

This fascinating first instalment of the Flashman Papers solves the mystery of what happened to Harry Flashman – that cad and bully from *Tom Brown's Schooldays* – after he was expelled from Rugby . . . here is the story of his early career in Lord Cardigan's 11th Light Dragoons, told by a self-confessed rotter, liar, womanizer and coward.

Fiction

☐	**The Chains of Fate**	Pamela Belle	£2.95p
☐	**Options**	Freda Bright	£1.50p
☐	**The Thirty-nine Steps**	John Buchan	£1.50p
☐	**Secret of Blackoaks**	Ashley Carter	£1.50p
☐	**Lovers and Gamblers**	Jackie Collins	£2.50p
☐	**My Cousin Rachel**	Daphne du Maurier	£2.50p
☐	**Flashman and the Redskins**	George Macdonald Fraser	£1.95p
☐	**The Moneychangers**	Arthur Hailey	£2.95p
☐	**Secrets**	Unity Hall	£2.50p
☐	**The Eagle Has Landed**	Jack Higgins	£1.95p
☐	**Sins of the Fathers**	Susan Howatch	£3.50p
☐	**Smiley's People**	John le Carré	£2.50p
☐	**To Kill a Mockingbird**	Harper Lee	£1.95p
☐	**Ghosts**	Ed McBain	£1.75p
☐	**The Silent People**	Walter Macken	£2.50p
☐	**Gone with the Wind**	Margaret Mitchell	£3.95p
☐	**Wilt**	Tom Sharpe	£1.95p
☐	**Rage of Angels**	Sidney Sheldon	£2.50p
☐	**The Unborn**	David Shobin	£1.50p
☐	**A Town Like Alice**	Nevile Shute	£2.50p
☐	**Gorky Park**	Martin Cruz Smith	£2.50p
☐	**A Falcon Flies**	Wilbur Smith	£2.50p
☐	**The Grapes of Wrath**	John Steinbeck	£2.50p
☐	**The Deep Well at Noon**	Jessica Stirling	£2.95p
☐	**The Ironmaster**	Jean Stubbs	£1.75p
☐	**The Music Makers**	E. V. Thompson	£2.50p

Non-fiction

☐	**The First Christian**	Karen Armstrong	£2.50p
☐	**Pregnancy**	Gordon Bourne	£3.95p
☐	**The Law is an Ass**	Gyles Brandreth	£1.75p
☐	**The 35mm Photographer's Handbook**	Julian Calder and John Garrett	£6.50p
☐	**London at its Best**	Hunter Davies	£2.90p
☐	**Back from the Brink**	Michael Edwardes	£2.95p

☐	**Travellers' Britain**	⎫ Arthur Eperon	£2.95p
☐	**Travellers' Italy**	⎭	£2.95p
☐	**The Complete Calorie Counter**	Eileen Fowler	90p
☐	**The Diary of Anne Frank**	Anne Frank	£1.75p
☐	**And the Walls Came Tumbling Down**	Jack Fishman	£1.95p
☐	**Linda Goodman's Sun Signs**	Linda Goodman	£2.95p
☐	**The Last Place on Earth**	Roland Huntford	£3.95p
☐	**Victoria RI**	Elizabeth Longford	£4.95p
☐	**Book of Worries**	Robert Morley	£1.50p
☐	**Airport International**	Brian Moynahan	£1.95p
☐	**Pan Book of Card Games**	Hubert Phillips	£1.95p
☐	**Keep Taking the Tabloids**	Fritz Spiegl	£1.75p
☐	**An Unfinished History of the World**	Hugh Thomas	£3.95p
☐	**The Baby and Child Book**	Penny and Andrew Stanway	£4.95p
☐	**The Third Wave**	Alvin Toffler	£2.95p
☐	**Pauper's Paris**	Miles Turner	£2.50p
☐	**The Psychic Detectives**	Colin Wilson	£2.50p

All these books are available at your local bookshop or newsagent, or can be ordered direct from the publisher. Indicate the number of copies required and fill in the form below   12

....

Name_____

(Block letters please)

Address_____

_____

Send to CS Department, Pan Books Ltd, PO Box 40, Basingstoke, Hants
Please enclose remittance to the value of the cover price plus:
35p for the first book plus 15p per copy for each additional book ordered
to a maximum charge of £1.25 to cover postage and packing
Applicable only in the UK

While every effort is made to keep prices low, it is sometimes
necessary to increase prices at short notice. Pan Books reserve
the right to show on covers and charge new retail prices which
may differ from those advertised in the text or elsewhere